D1594126

# Soufflés
# Quiches
# Mousses

## &

## THE RANDOM EGG

**Other cookbooks by George Bradshaw**

COOK UNTIL DONE  (with Ruth Norman)

SUPPERS AND MIDNIGHT SNACKS

COOKING AT THE TABLE

# George Bradshaw

# Soufflés Quiches Mousses

**& THE RANDOM EGG**

HARPER & ROW, PUBLISHERS
New York, Evanston, San Francisco, London

Portions of this book previously appeared in *Vogue* and *Playboy* magazines.

FIRST EDITION

STANDARD BOOK NUMBER: 06-010451-1

LIBRARY OF CONGRESS CATALOG CARD NUMBER: 78-156508

# Contents

# The Stampede
# Into the Kitchen
# Examined

Leisure threatens us more and more. The four-day week is already here. The three-day week stands menacingly dead ahead. Within sight is the gloomy sublimity of the two-day, the one-day. Time is no longer of the essence; it has become the dark and burdensome mass.

Of course, we who once reveled in the flight of time, we do what we can. We take up needlepoint, we build catamarans in the garage, we thumb through tropic islands, we protest, we communicate, we have opinions on everything, we make mosaic ashtrays, and we drink.

We turn to the arts. We inundate museums, we overflow concert halls, we real billions of books, we even, God help us, go to the theatre.

But it all just isn't enough, is it? Time still hangs heavy.

The Industry of Leisure, that conglomerate of conglomerates, is failing us. It has come to our attention that all this going to Byzantium or West Palm Beach, this painting of pictures with numbers on them, this consideration of the art of Jean-Luc Godard even, is not the whole story.

I know a quite decent man who, within memory, had never

been inside a kitchen, but now finds himself as a matter of course up to his elbows once a week in stone-ground flour, making bread.

We are a practical people. For all that has happened, we are still an Acres of Diamonds bunch, and even if momentarily giddied by an hourglass gone berserk, we eventually remember the riches in our back yard.

It looks very much as if those riches are turning out to be Ris de Veau Financière.

The stampede in the kitchen these last few years has been nothing short of appalling. Once upon a time—do you remember?—the kitchen was a room that was mostly deserted, lit unappealingly by one hanging bulb, adorned by an oil-cloth-covered table, its only sound a ticking clock.

But now . . . It has been transformed into the most perfect machine for killing time ever invented by man. It has been made handsome and comfortable with easy chairs and sofas and pretty colors and flattering lights. There are music and television. The stove is now a juke box (bells ring, lights flash). Dishes wash themselves, garbage disappears. A dozen electrical conveniences whir and clatter and buzz and hum. The clock is silent. There are a desk and a telephone. The *batterie* hangs upon the walls, gleaming; it boasts everything from a truffle cutter to a salamander. The shelves and refrigerators hold promises of elaborate delights. There is a bar.

It is the center of the house. Father's workshop, with its cunning devices for cutting up pieces of wood, once so necessary, stands deserted. The "family room," with its dart board, lies under a film of dust; even the electric hedge cutter out in the garage is getting rusty.

I wonder if this abandoning of old toys in the rush to the kitchen does not have some further meaning than just one more smothering of boredom? Maybe a moral meaning?

We as a people are feeling guilty, I think you will agree. It is a new feeling for us—we never had time before—but it is rising. If leisure didn't give it to us, at least leisure gave us the chance to nurture it.

It is new and it is rising, our guilt. Do you not think it pertinent that this rising sense of guilt coincides almost exactly with the rising return of our nation to the kitchen?

Can the kitchen, like patriotism, be the last refuge of us scoundrels? Is it the sanctuary we flee to from a world where you can't buy a share of bank stock without condoning something, or have your hair cut without offending someone?

Its moral position is impeccable, certainly. No one can fault you for adding to the happiness of mankind by baking an apple pie.

The stampede has changed the reading habits of the nation, for sure.

Once upon a time—in that kitchen with the oilcloth-covered table—a single cookbook did the trick. It lay tucked away in a drawer under the tea towels, but it was little used: every cook *had* her repertory and was suspicious of innovation.

But now. There are more books in the kitchen than there are in the library. Everything from three-volume encyclopedias to four-page giveaways from chutney manufacturers.

Shelf after shelf after shelf: Chinese, Mexican, Norwegian, Italian, French.

All secrets have been discovered. Let a Peruvian peasant do something edible to an unripe banana, and the word is instantly broadcast—and copyrighted. Poor Escoffier has no surprises left: he's available in Braille. Every breeze that blew in Burgundy in 1952 has been carefully recorded. The recipe for the Queen of England's liver and onions is yours for the asking.

Indeed, cookbooks outsell sex books. I will not say have replaced them, but it is true that "tumescent" is nowadays a term we apply (hopefully, as before) to soufflés.


"Everything in this world has its particular moment," said the Cardinal de Retz, and high on his list of everything must have been eggs.

No other sort of food, in the cooking, so demands that you keep an eye on it. Like everything else in the kitchen, the care of an egg is a matter of practice, so here is a book that concentrates primarily on what to do with an egg. There are some other recipes: a number of the eggs have a menu pendant, and when these include a dish that might be unfamiliar it is cross-referenced to a final chapter, The Additional Recipes.

# Soufflés

Soufflés are much maligned dishes. "Difficult," "chancy," "maybe" you hear about them: well, nonsense; they are infinitely easier to make than a common stew.

There is only one inflexible rule about a soufflé; it must be eaten when ready. A soufflé will not wait upon people: people must wait upon a soufflé.

You will benefit, I think, by reading the following paragraphs before you plunge into any of the recipes. They will give you some insight into *why* you are doing *what* you are doing—a very comforting feeling for anyone who finds himself alone in a kitchen with his first soufflé.

*The Soufflé Dish:* You can make a soufflé in any heat-proof utensil of no more than two-quart capacity. It is good, however, to use the traditional French white china dish; it makes the soufflé look better when it comes to the table. I have specified almost always a two-quart dish because with it you do not need a collar—that piece of paper tied around the rim of the dish to prevent the soufflé from running over. I find using collars a pretentious nuisance, about on a par with binding the feet of Chinese girl babies.

All of these recipes are for four people. (Some of the recipes for accompanying dishes—the veal, the lamb—will serve more.) You may halve any of them and use a one-quart dish. Under no circumstance attempt to double or triple a recipe and try to cook it in a big bowl. It will not work. Make instead two or three soufflés of the usual size. It is useful to have a one-and-a-half-quart dish also. There are several soufflés—lemon, for instance, and tomato—which for some reason are reluctant to rise very high. They look more successful, therefore, in a one-and-a-half-quart dish.

If you wish to serve individual soufflés—clam, for instance, makes a good first course—there are small-size dishes, about eight-ounce.

Of course, I am speaking above of the classic and, I think, best way of serving a soufflé. But actually they can be cooked in almost anything—half an orange rind, a scallop shell, a baked-potato skin, inside a crepe, indeed even on a flat plate.

*Preparation of the Dish:* The soufflé dish should be rubbed with butter, bottom and sides. For entrée and vegetable soufflés, sprinkle a little flour over the butter. For dessert soufflés, sprinkle with a little sugar.

And, if sometime you should forget to do this, it really won't matter.

*Egg Whites:* The whites of eggs should be beaten until they are stiff and creamy. They should not be overbeaten until they are hard and dry. If you use a hand beater you don't need to worry about this advice because you will probably be exhausted long before the whites are hard and dry.

But there is a reason for this warning for anyone who might be too ambitious with an electric mixer. If the whites are too stiff they simply will not combine easily and thoroughly with the sauce. So watch for the right moment: the whites will be ready when they glisten and stand in peaks.

In each one of the recipes you will notice that a large spoonful of whites is folded into the sauce *before* this sauce is dribbled into the remaining whites. *Don't* neglect to do this. It lightens the sauce—aerates it—so that you do not have the dead weight of a heavy mixture dropping—plunk—on the bubbles of egg whites.

*Cream of Tartar:* You will notice that a half teaspoon of cream of tartar is included in all the following recipes. You are instructed to sprinkle it over the egg whites as they are being beaten.

A veteran soufflé maker will likely ignore the instruction, but the recruit will do well to follow it. For cream of tartar is insurance—like a major medical policy, which you may never need, but which is comforting to have around; it stiffens the backbone of the egg whites, guarantees that they do what they are supposed to do, rise and shine.

*Cooling:* This is one of the real requirements of soufflé making. The sauce must, no kidding, be cool.

A good way to determine this right temperature is to hold the top of your double boiler in the palm of your hand. If you can do this comfortably, the sauce is cool.

*Cooking:* In all the recipes I say a 350° oven. It must always be preheated.

About cooking time: it certainly varies. I have made numberless soufflés that were ready in twenty-five minutes. On the other hand I have encountered recalcitrant soufflés, made of the same recipes, cooked in the same oven, that demanded thirty minutes.

So I have discovered a method for testing. A soufflé, so long as it remains in its warm oven home, is a pretty sturdy dish. You don't have to worry about tiptoeing around the kitchen or opening the oven door and taking a look.

At about minute twenty-two, I open the oven door and give the dish a little shove. If the top of the soufflé shakes only slightly I know it is a well-mannered soufflé and will be done in two or three minutes. If, on the other hand, the crust really trembles, so that I have the feeling that the underneath is still soupy, I recognize a delinquent, which will require another eight or even ten minutes.

After you have done this test on several soufflés you will find yourself able to judge the degree of doneness exactly.

NOTE: All the recipes will make six or eight individual soufflés, depending on the size of your cocottes or ramekins. Naturally, the baking time is shorter. Twelve to fifteen minutes will do it, but test, as with large ones.

# Soufflés as
# Main Dishes

*The perfect lunch takes place out of doors on a fine day under a shady tree. And this is what you should have: a Cheese Soufflé, a salad of young greens, fresh sweet strawberries, and homemade brownies.*

## Cheese Soufflé I

3 tablespoons butter
3 tablespoons flour
1 cup milk
½ pound sharp Cheddar
    cheese, grated

Dash of cayenne pepper
6 eggs, separated
½ teaspoon cream of tartar

In the top part of a double boiler (over boiling water) melt the butter, stir in the flour, and cook for a couple of minutes, then add the milk and the cheese, and stirring constantly, cook until the mixture is thick and smooth, about five minutes. Remove the top part of the double boiler from the heat, add a dash of cayenne and the egg yolks, and beat until all is smooth. Allow the mixture to cool, fifteen minutes at least.

Beat the egg whites until they are stiff and creamy. Sprinkle the cream of tartar over them as you beat.

When the cheese mixture is cool, spoon about one-third of the egg whites into it and combine vigorously. Now dribble this mixture over the remaining egg whites and lift and fold carefully until all is combined.

Slide this mixture into a buttered and floured two-quart soufflé dish and place in a preheated 350° oven.

This should be done in about twenty-five minutes, but test it as suggested on page 12.

## Cheese Soufflé II

3 tablespoons butter
3 tablespoons flour
1 tablespoon curry powder
1 cup milk
½ pound sharp Cheddar cheese, grated

½ tablespoon finely chopped mango chutney
6 eggs, separated
½ teaspoon cream of tartar

In the top part of a double boiler (over boiling water) melt the butter, stir in the flour and the curry powder and cook for a couple of minutes, then add the milk and the cheese. Stirring constantly, cook until the mixture is thick and smooth, about five minutes. Remove the top part of the double boiler from the heat, add the mango chutney and the egg yolks and beat until all is smooth. Allow the mixture to cool, fifteen minutes at least.

Beat the egg whites until they are stiff and creamy. Sprinkle the cream of tartar over them as you beat.

When the cheese mixture is cool, spoon about one-third of the egg whites into it and combine vigorously. Now dribble this mixture over the remaining egg whites and lift and fold carefully until all is combined.

Slide this mixture into a buttered and floured two-quart soufflé dish and place in a preheated 350° oven.

This should be done in about twenty-five minutes, but test it.

# Anchovy Soufflé

*With this soufflé try an Onion-and-Cucumber Aspic (page 125) and a slice of ripe Camembert.*

| | |
|---|---|
| 1 two-ounce can of anchovies with capers and olive oil (or 1½ tablespoons of anchovy paste) | 3 tablespoons flour |
| | 1 cup chicken broth |
| | 4 egg yolks |
| | 5 egg whites |
| 3 tablespoons butter | ½ teaspoon cream of tartar |

Put the anchovies into a bowl and mash them with a wooden spoon, capers and all, into a paste.

In the top part of a double boiler (over boiling water) melt the butter, stir in the flour, and cook for a couple of minutes, then add the chicken broth, and stirring constantly, cook until the mixture is thick and smooth, about five minutes. Remove the top part of the double boiler from the heat, add the anchovy paste and egg yolks, and beat until all is smooth. Allow the mixture to cool, fifteen minutes at least.

Beat the egg whites until they are stiff and creamy. Sprinkle the cream of tartar over them as you beat.

When the anchovy mixture is cool, spoon about one-third of the egg whites into it and combine vigorously. Now dribble this mixture over the remaining egg whites and lift and fold carefully until all is combined.

Slide this mixture into a buttered and floured two-quart soufflé dish and place in a preheated 350° oven.

This should be done in about twenty-five minutes, but test it.

# Lobster Soufflé

*This dish is rather rich, so you had best keep the other food simple: a Belgian Endive Salad (page 71) and for dessert lime sherbet with vanilla wafers will be enough.*

3 tablespoons butter
3 tablespoons flour
½ cup light cream
½ cup chicken broth
1 cup freshly grated Parmesan cheese
6 eggs, separated

1 pound cooked fresh lobster meat cut in manageable pieces
2 tablespoons sherry
2 extra tablespoons cream
½ teaspoon paprika
½ teaspoon cream of tartar

In the top part of a double boiler (over boiling water) melt the butter, add the flour, mix to a smooth paste, and cook a minute. Add the half cup of cream and the chicken broth. When this barely begins to thicken, add the cheese; cook until mixture is smooth and thick. Remove from heat and beat in the egg yolks. Allow to cool.

In a bowl place the lobster meat plus two tablespoons of the cheese mixture, the sherry and the two extra tablespoons cream. Douse with paprika. Mix and heat thoroughly and place in a two-quart buttered and floured soufflé dish.

Beat the egg whites until they are stiff and creamy, simultaneously sprinkling the cream of tartar into them. Spoon about a quarter of them into the cheese mixture and beat until well combined. Dribble this mixture slowly over the remaining egg whites, lifting and folding carefully.

Pour this mixture over the lobster and place in a preheated 350° oven. Bake for about twenty-five minutes.

# Clam Soufflé

*This makes an excellent first course, which can be made in individual servings or in one dish. Afterward you might have cold chicken legs, Pickled Beets (page 72) and homemade applesauce.*

| | |
|---|---|
| 2 seven-ounce cans minced clams | Dash of cayenne pepper |
| 5 egg yolks | 6 egg whites |
| | ½ teaspoon cream of tartar |

Drain practically all the juice from the clams. In a bowl combine the clams with the egg yolks and the dash of cayenne pepper.

In a separate bowl, beat the egg whites until they are stiff and creamy. Sprinkle the cream of tartar over them as you beat.

Spoon about one-third of the egg whites into the clam mixture and combine vigorously. Now dribble this mixture over the remaining egg whites and lift and fold carefully until all is combined.

Slide this mixture into a buttered and floured two-quart soufflé dish and place in a preheated 350° oven.

This should be done in about twenty-five minutes, but test it.

# Tomato-Shrimp Soufflé

*Something bland and pleasant to have with this soufflé is a Fresh Mushroom Salad (page 72) with water biscuits and cold fresh pears for dessert.*

| | |
|---|---|
| 3 tablespoons butter | 6 egg whites |
| 3 tablespoons flour | ½ teaspoon cream of tartar |
| 1½ cups tomato-vegetable juice (V-8, for instance) | 16 cooked, shelled and deveined medium shrimps |
| 3 tablespoons grated Parmesan cheese | 2 tablespoons hot cocktail sauce (the sort with horseradish in it) |
| 4 egg yolks, beaten | |

In the top part of a double boiler (over boiling water) melt the butter, stir in the flour, and cook for a few minutes. Add the tomato-vegetable juice and Parmesan cheese. Stirring constantly, cook the mixture until it is thick and creamy. This should take about five minutes.

Remove top part of double boiler from the heat and add the beaten egg yolks. Stir vigorously until the sauce is smooth. Allow to cool completely.

Beat the egg whites into stiff, moist peaks, sprinkling the cream of tartar over as you beat. Spoon a third of the whites over the tomato sauce and combine thoroughly. Dribble this over the remaining whites. Fold and lift carefully until all is blended lightly.

Mix the shrimps with the cocktail sauce, heat, and put into the bottom of a buttered and floured two-quart soufflé dish. Pour the tomato mixture over the shrimps.

Bake in a preheated 350° oven for twenty-five minutes. Test to be certain the soufflé is done before removing it from the oven.

# Sole Soufflé

*Serve with this fresh green peas, cooked in the French way with a little lettuce and a couple of white onions, and for dessert have Baked Bananas in Honey and Chutney (page 134).*

| | |
|---|---|
| 4 equal-size fillets of sole | 1 cup freshly grated Parmesan |
| Juice of ½ lemon |    cheese |
| 3 tablespoons butter | 4 egg yolks, beaten |
| 3 tablespoons flour | 5 egg whites |
| 1 cup chicken broth | ½ teaspoon cream of tartar |
| Dash of salt and pepper | |

Roll each of the sole fillets up neatly and fasten with a toothpick. Poach them gently in simmering water to which you have added the lemon juice. When they are done—seven or eight minutes—remove them carefully and let them drain on absorbent paper.

When the fillets have drained, place them on their sides in the bottom of a buttered and floured two-quart soufflé dish. Remove the toothpicks. Keep warm.

In the top part of a double boiler (over boiling water) melt the butter; stir in the flour. Cook for a couple of minutes. Pour in the chicken broth, add a dash of salt and pepper and the Parmesan cheese. Stir constantly until mixture is thick and smooth.

Remove the top part of the double boiler from the heat and then add beaten egg yolks. Again, stir until smooth. Then set aside to cool for at least fifteen minutes.

Beat the egg whites, sprinkling the cream of tartar over them as you beat, into stiff, creamy peaks.

Spoon a third of the beaten whites over the cooled cheese

mixture. Stir in vigorously. Then dribble this sauce over the rest of the whites. Lift and fold carefully until all is blended lightly.

Slide this over the sole fillets. Bake in a preheated 350° oven for twenty-five minutes, but test before removing from oven.


## Ham Soufflé

*Good with this are Cold Curried Apples (page 133), hot rusks, and for dessert lemon sherbet with extra lemon juice squeezed over it.*

| | |
|---|---|
| 3 tablespoons butter | 6 ounce can or jar Smithfield ham spread |
| 3 tablespoons flour | |
| 1 cup chicken broth | 6 egg whites |
| ½ cup grated Parmesan cheese | ½ teaspoon cream of tartar |
| 5 egg yolks, beaten | |

In the top part of a double boiler (over boiling water) melt the butter, stir in the flour, and cook for a couple of minutes. Add the chicken broth and Parmesan cheese. Stirring constantly, cook until the mixture is thick and smooth—about five minutes. Remove top part of the double boiler from the heat, add the egg yolks and the Smithfield ham spread, and beat until the sauce is smooth. Allow this to cool for at least fifteen minutes.

Beat the egg whites until they are stiff and creamy, adding the cream of tartar while you are beating the whites.

Spoon a third of the beaten whites into the ham mixture and combine vigorously. Dribble this over the remaining whites and lift and fold carefully to combine evenly and lightly.

Pour this into a buttered and floured two-quart soufflé dish and place in a preheated 350° oven for about twenty-five minutes.

# Lamb Curry Soufflé

*Wild rice seems the natural accompaniment to this soufflé. Have also cucumbers vinaigrette. And for the dessert: big red apples.*

3 tablespoons butter
3 tablespoons flour
1 cup chicken broth
1 tablespoon curry powder
1 cup ground cooked lamb (in coarsest blade of meat grinder)

5 eggs, separated
½ teaspoon cream of tartar
2 tablespoons Major Grey's chutney

In the top part of a double boiler (over boiling water) melt the butter, stir in the flour, and cook for a couple of minutes, then add the chicken broth and the curry powder, and stirring constantly, cook until the mixture is thick and smooth, about five minutes. Remove the top part of the double boiler from the heat, add the lamb and the egg yolks, and beat until all is smooth. Allow the mixture to cool, fifteen minutes at least.

Beat the egg whites until they are stiff and creamy. Sprinkle the cream of tartar over them as you beat.

When the yolk mixture is cool, spoon about one-third of the egg whites into it and combine vigorously. Now dribble this mixture over the remaining egg whites and lift and fold carefully until all is combined.

Slide one-half the mixture into a buttered and floured two-quart soufflé dish, then dot the chutney over this in the middle of the soufflé and pour over the other half of the mixture. Place the dish in a preheated 350° oven.

This should be done in about twenty-five minutes, but test it.

# Ground-Sirloin Soufflé

*This must be served with Horseradish Sherbet (page 126). Also have sliced fresh tomatoes in an oil-and-vinegar dressing, sprinkled with fresh dill. A gooey chocolate cake makes a good dessert.*

| | |
|---|---|
| 3 tablespoons butter | Freshly ground black pepper |
| 3 tablespoons flour | ½ pound ground sirloin |
| 1 cup beef bouillon | Additional butter |
| 3 tablespoons grated Parmesan | 5 eggs, separated |
| 1 tablespoon Worcestershire or A-1 sauce | ½ teaspoon cream of tartar |

In the top part of a double boiler (over boiling water) melt the three tablespoons butter, add the flour, mix, and allow to cook a minute. Pour in the beef bouillon gradually and cook, stirring constantly, until the sauce is thick. Then add the cheese, the Worcestershire or A-1 sauce, and some freshly ground black pepper. Remove from heat.

Now crumble the ground sirloin into a skillet with a little butter, push it around until it is browned, and add to the sauce. Next add the beaten yolks of the eggs. Return to heat for just a moment, then take it off the fire, and beat it well. Allow to cool.

Beat the egg whites until they are stiff and creamy. Sprinkle the cream of tartar over them as you beat.

When the yolk mixture is cool, spoon about one-third of the egg whites into it and combine vigorously. Now dribble this mixture over the remaining egg whites and lift and fold carefully.

Slide this mixture into a buttered and floured two-quart soufflé dish and place in a preheated 350° oven for twenty-five minutes or a little longer. This soufflé should be firm.

# Plain Soufflé with Caviar Sauce

*This is a soufflé to have some happy midnight when you are cele-brating something fine. A bottle of champagne is really all you need to go with it.*

FOR THE SOUFFLÉ:
3 tablespoons butter
3 tablespoons flour
1½ cups milk
4 tablespoons grated Parmesan
    cheese
Cayenne pepper

6 egg yolks, beaten
6 egg whites
½ teaspoon cream of tartar

FOR THE SAUCE:
4-ounce jar best black caviar
3 tablespoons sour cream

Melt the butter in the top part of a double boiler (over boiling water). Stir in the flour and cook for a few minutes. Add the milk and the Parmesan cheese and, stirring constantly, cook until all is smooth. Remove top part of the double boiler from the heat, add a dash of cayenne and the beaten egg yolks. Stir until this becomes a creamy sauce, then set aside to cool to room tempera-ture.

Mix the caviar with the sour cream and refrigerate.

Beat the egg whites, sprinkling the cream of tartar over them, until they form moist peaks. Spoon one-third of these beaten whites into the basic sauce and mix well. Dribble this over the remaining whites and lift and fold gently to combine throughout.

Slide this mixture into a buttered and floured two-quart soufflé dish and bake in a preheated 350° oven. The dish should be done in twenty-five minutes, but test ahead of time to make certain.

When serving the soufflé, dribble some of the caviar and sour cream sauce over each portion.

# Four Breakfast Soufflés

Here are four breakfast soufflés. Not, naturally, for early-morning breakfast when someone has to catch the 7:32, but for lazy Saturdays and Sundays when time doesn't matter.

## Bacon-and-Eggs Soufflé

3 tablespoons butter
3 tablespoons flour
1½ cups well-seasoned chicken broth

5 eggs, separated
10 strips crisp bacon, crumbled
½ teaspoon cream of tartar

In the top part of a double boiler (over boiling water) melt the butter. Stir in the flour and cook for a few minutes. Add the chicken broth and cook, stirring constantly, until the mixture is thick and smooth.

Remove the top part of the double boiler from the heat. Let

the mixture cool a bit and then add the beaten egg yolks and three-quarters of the crisp crumbled bacon.

Let the mixture cool thoroughly.

Beat the egg whites until they are stiff and creamy. Sprinkle the cream of tartar over them as you beat.

After the mixture has cooled, spoon about one-third of the whites into it and combine vigorously. Dribble this mixture over the remaining whites, lifting and folding carefully until all is combined.

Place the mixture in a buttered and floured two-quart soufflé dish. Sprinkle the remaining crumbled bacon on top of the soufflé.

Bake for about twenty-five minutes in a preheated 350° oven. Test to be certain it is done.

# Chipped-Beef Soufflé

*While you are waiting for the soufflé to bake have whatever is the best fresh fruit at the moment. You will want it with lots of hot buttered toast or croissants and a variety of jams, or, better still, some sharp piccalilli, and of course strong black coffee.*

| | |
|---|---|
| Small jar chipped beef (2½ ounces) | 1½ cups milk |
| | 5 eggs, separated |
| 3 tablespoons butter | ¼ cup sherry |
| 3 tablespoons flour | ½ teaspoon cream of tartar |

Wash the chipped beef if it is too salty. Shred it with scissors.

In the top part of a double boiler (over boiling water) melt the butter. Stir in the flour and cook for a few minutes. Add the milk. Cook the mixture, stirring constantly, until it is thick and smooth.

Remove the top part of the double boiler from the fire and add the shredded chipped beef. Beat the egg yolks into the mixture until amalgamated. Add the sherry. Set this aside to cool for about fifteen minutes.

Beat the egg whites until they are stiff but still creamy. Sprinkle the cream of tartar over them as you beat.

When the chipped-beef mixture has cooled completely, spoon about one-third of the whites over it and fold in vigorously. Then dribble this mixture over the remaining egg whites and fold in carefully until all is combined.

Slide all this into a buttered and floured two-quart soufflé dish. Place in a preheated 350° oven for approximately twenty-five minutes. Test to be certain the soufflé is done.

# Blueberry Buckwheat Soufflé

| | |
|---|---|
| 3 tablespoons butter | 6 egg whites |
| 4 tablespoons buckwheat flour | ½ teaspoon cream of tartar |
| 1¼ cups milk | 1 cup blueberries very lightly |
| 2 tablespoons sugar |    floured |
| 4 egg yolks | Honey |

In the top part of a double boiler (over boiling water) melt the butter. Stir in the buckwheat flour and cook for a few minutes. Add the milk and sugar. Stir constantly and cook for about five minutes until the mixture is thick and smooth.

Remove the top part of the double boiler from the heat and allow to cool for a couple of minutes. Beat the egg yolks and add to mixture, stirring constantly until all is blended. Then allow mixture to cool for about fifteen minutes.

Beat the egg whites until they reach stiff, creamy peaks, sprinkling in the cream of tartar as you beat.

After yolk mixture has cooled sufficiently, add lightly floured blueberries. Then spoon about a third of the beaten egg whites into the mixture and combine vigorously. When the mixture appears properly aerated, dribble it over the remaining egg whites and lift and fold carefully until all is combined.

Pour the blueberry mixture into a buttered and floured two-quart soufflé dish. Place in a preheated 350° oven and bake for at least thirty minutes. This soufflé should be definitely firm.

Let each eater spoon honey over his portion.

# Cornmeal Soufflé

2 cups milk
⅓ cup yellow cornmeal
1 tablespoon butter
Salt and pepper

4 egg yolks
5 egg whites
½ teaspoon cream of tartar

In a saucepan heat the milk almost to a boil.

Keeping the flame low, gradually add the cornmeal, butter, salt, and pepper. Stir constantly and cook until this forms a thin gruel. Then remove from the flame.

Beat the egg yolks and stir into the cornmeal mixture thoroughly. Allow this to cool for about fifteen minutes.

Sprinkle cream of tartar over the egg whites while beating them into creamy peaks. Combine a third of the beaten whites with the cornmeal so that you have a foamy sauce. Dribble this sauce over the remaining whites. Lift and fold carefully.

Slip this into a buttered and floured two-quart soufflé dish and place in a preheated 350° oven.

The cooking time is approximately twenty minutes, but do test it.

# Vegetable Soufflés

### Corn Soufflé

*This is a fine dish to have with Crab Louis (page 127). Finish off the meal with a big slice of ripe watermelon.*

2 cups fresh cooked corn, grated from the cob (or a 16-ounce can cream-style corn)
½ cup milk

2 teaspoons sugar
4 egg yolks, beaten
½ teaspoon cream of tartar
6 egg whites

Cook the corn on the cob until it is just tender. Then cool and grate the ears. You need two cups of the grated corn. Add in the milk and sugar to the fresh corn. (If canned corn is used, omit milk and sugar.)

Mix in with this (or the can of cream-style corn) the beaten egg yolks. Beat until smooth.

Sprinkle the cream of tartar over the egg whites as you beat them into stiff, creamy peaks. Stir in vigorously a third of the whites with the corn sauce and then dribble this over the remaining whites. Lift and fold carefully to combine well.

Slip this into a buttered and floured two-quart soufflé dish and place in a preheated 350° oven.

The soufflé should be done in twenty-five minutes, but, of course, test it.

## Cucumber Soufflé

*This is a good thing to have with cold salmon mayonnaise, and then a bowl of fresh raspberries with cream.*

| | |
|---|---|
| 1½ medium-sized cucumbers | Additional butter |
| 1 cup chicken broth | Salt and pepper |
| 3 tablespoons butter | 6 egg whites |
| 3 tablespoons flour | ½ teaspoon cream of tartar |
| 5 egg yolks | |

Peel and chop one-half cucumber. Place it in a blender with the chicken broth and run until all is liquid.

In the top part of a double boiler (over boiling water) melt the three tablespoons butter, stir in the flour, and cook for a couple of minutes, then add the chicken broth from the blender, and stirring constantly, cook until the mixture is thick and smooth, about five minutes. Remove the top part of the double boiler from the heat, add the egg yolks and beat until all is smooth. Allow the mixture to cool, fifteen minutes at least.

Peel and slice crosswise a whole cucumber; simmer for five

minutes in water to cover. Drain, coat with a little butter and salt and pepper. Place these in the bottom of a two-quart buttered soufflé dish. Keep warm.

Beat the egg whites until they are stiff and creamy. Sprinkle the cream of tartar over them as you beat.

When the chicken-broth mixture has cooled, spoon about one-third of the egg whites into it and combine vigorously. Now dribble this mixture over the remaining egg whites and lift and fold carefully until all is combined.

Slide this mixture into the soufflé dish on top of the sliced cucumbers and place in a preheated 350° oven.

This should be done in about twenty-five minutes, but test it.

## Tomato Soufflé

*Arrange a platter of prosciutto or Westphalian ham on a bed of lettuce to serve with this soufflé. For dessert have slices of good cold melon.*

| | |
|---|---|
| 6 medium-sized tomatoes | 2 tablespoons tomato sauce |
| Butter | Salt and pepper |
| 3 tablespoons flour | 5 eggs, separated |
| 1 cup milk | ½ teaspoon cream of tartar |
| 3 tablespoons grated Parmesan cheese | |

Chop up the tomatoes. Put a little butter in a pan and cook them over lowish heat. As they soften, stir and mash them. The idea is to drive the water off, and they will be done when they "blop" instead of boil—this may take twenty minutes. Now push them through a sieve to get rid of the skins and seeds.

In the top part of a double boiler (over boiling water) melt three tablespoons butter, stir in the flour, and cook for a couple of minutes, then add the milk and the cheese, the tomato sauce, and the tomato purée, and stirring constantly, cook until the mixture is thick and smooth, about five minutes. Remove the top part of the double boiler from the heat, add a bit of salt and pepper and the egg yolks, and beat until all is smooth. Allow the mixture to cool, fifteen minutes at least.

Beat the egg whites until they are stiff and creamy. Sprinkle the cream of tartar over them as you beat.

When the tomato mixture is cool, spoon about one-third of the egg whites into it and combine vigorously. Now dribble this mixture over the remaining egg whites and lift and fold carefully until all is combined.

Slide this mixture into a buttered and floured two-quart soufflé dish and place in a preheated 350° oven.

This should be done in about twenty-five minutes, but test it.

*With slices of cold leftover turkey and a cranberry-orange sauce either of the following two Sweet-Potato Soufflés does well. For dessert, serve seedless white grapes rolled in beaten egg whites, then in powdered sugar, and chilled well.*

## Sweet-Potato Soufflé I

| | |
|---|---|
| 2 cups mashed sweet potato | 4 egg yolks |
| 2 tablespoons butter | 6 egg whites |
| ¾ cup milk | ½ teaspoon cream of tartar |
| 1 teaspoon grated nutmeg | 1 tablespoon dark-brown sugar |
| Dash of salt and pepper | 1 teaspoon grated lemon rind |

If you have some easy way to make smooth mashed sweet potatoes from scratch, do it. Otherwise, buy canned cooked ones, drain and rinse them, and put through a potato ricer. You need two cups.

In the top part of a double boiler melt the butter (over boiling water). Stir in the milk, the nutmeg, and a dash of salt and pepper. Blend in the mashed sweet potato. Cook the mixture for about five minutes, stirring constantly.

Remove the top part of double boiler from the heat and beat in the egg yolks. Stir until all is smooth.

Allow this mixture to cool for about fifteen minutes.

Beat the egg whites into stiff, creamy peaks. Sprinkle the cream of tartar over them as you beat.

Combine a third of the beaten whites with the cooled sweet-potato sauce. After you have mixed this thoroughly, dribble it over the remaining egg whites. Lift and fold carefully until all is blended.

Pour this into a buttered and floured two-quart soufflé dish. Sprinkle brown sugar and lemon rind on top.

Bake in a preheated 350° oven for twenty-five minutes. Test the soufflé for doneness before taking it from the oven.

## Sweet-Potato Soufflé II

2 tablespoons butter
1 cup applesauce
2 teaspoons lemon juice
1 teaspoon grated nutmeg

2 cups mashed sweet potato
4 egg yolks, beaten
6 egg whites
½ teaspoon cream of tartar

Melt the butter in the top part of a double boiler, stir in the applesauce, lemon juice, nutmeg, and sweet potato. Stirring constantly, cook this mixture for about five minutes until all blends smoothly.

Allow to cool for a few minutes and then add the beaten egg yolks. Again, stir until all is smooth.

Cool this mixture for at least fifteen minutes.

Beat the egg whites, sprinkling in the cream of tartar as you beat them. After the sweet-potato mixture has cooled, mix in vigorously one-third of the stiff egg whites. Then dribble this sauce over the remaining egg whites and lift and fold carefully until all is combined.

Slide the mixture into a buttered and floured two-quart soufflé dish and place in a preheated 350° oven.

Bake for approximately twenty-five minutes. Test to be certain it is done.

*Either of these two Potato Soufflés will add a certain zest to a simple winter dinner of broiled lamb chops and fresh green beans. For dessert, make it easy: coffee ice cream.*

## Potato Soufflé I

| | |
|---|---|
| 4 medium-size Idaho baking potatoes | 1 tablespoon anchovy paste |
| 2 tablespoons butter | 4 egg yolks |
| 1 cup milk | 6 egg whites |
| | ½ teaspoon cream of tartar |

Bake the potatoes until done. Cut a neat oval strip out of each and scoop out the innards. Beat the potato pulp with the butter and milk until it is smooth.

Add the anchovy paste and egg yolks. Stir this mixture until smooth. Allow it to cool for at least fifteen minutes.

Beat the whites of eggs until they form stiff, creamy peaks. Sprinkle the cream of tartar over them as you beat.

Fold in vigorously one-third of the egg whites to the potato mixture. When this appears completely aerated, dribble it over the remaining egg whites. Lift and fold carefully until all combines.

You may pile this back either into the four shells, in which case they will need fifteen to eighteen minutes to puff up in a preheated 350° oven, or into a buttered and floured two-quart soufflé dish, which will require about twenty-five minutes.

Test to see if the soufflé is done before removing from oven.

# Potato Soufflé II

| | |
|---|---|
| 2 tablespoons butter | 2 cups mashed potatoes |
| 1 cup milk | 4 egg yolks |
| Dash of salt and pepper | 6 egg whites |
| 1 cup freshly grated Parmesan cheese | ½ teaspoon cream of tartar |

In the top part of a double boiler (over boiling water) melt the butter and stir in the milk. Add a dash of salt and pepper and two-thirds cup of the freshly grated Parmesan cheese. Cook this for a few minutes until it has combined thoroughly.

Remove the top part of the double boiler from the heat. Add in the mashed potatoes. Cool the mixture for a few minutes and then beat in the egg yolks. Stir until smooth.

Set this aside to cool for fifteen minutes at least.

Beat the egg whites into stiff, creamy peaks, sprinkling the cream of tartar over them as you beat.

When the potato mixture has cooled completely, fold in vigorously one-third of the beaten egg whites. Then dribble this over the remaining egg whites and fold and lift carefully until all is combined.

Slide this mixture into a buttered and floured two-quart soufflé dish. Sprinkle the remaining one-third cup grated Parmesan over it.

Cook in a preheated 350° oven for twenty-five minutes. Test before removing from the oven.

# Onion Soufflé

*This one is good with the best hamburgers, a tossed green salad, and a board of various cheeses.*

| | |
|---|---|
| 2 large strong onions | Scant teaspoon freshly ground |
| ½ cup sour cream | white pepper |
| 3 tablespoons butter | 4 egg yolks |
| 3 tablespoons flour | 6 egg whites |
| ½ cup beef bouillon | ½ teaspoon cream of tartar |
| Scant teaspoon salt | |

Peel and chop the onions. Purée in a blender with the sour cream. You should have a cup and a half in all.

In the top part of a double boiler (over boiling water) melt the butter. Stir in the flour and cook for a few minutes. Add the beef bouillon and the salt and pepper. Stir constantly and cook for about five minutes until the mixture is thick and smooth.

Remove from the heat. Beat in the onion and sour cream purée. Allow this to cool for a minute and then beat in the egg yolks.

This mixture should cool to room temperature, which will take at least fifteen minutes.

Beat the whites of eggs until they form stiff, creamy peaks. Sprinkle the cream of tartar over them as you beat.

Fold in one-third of the beaten whites to the onion mixture. Combine vigorously. Then dribble this over the remaining egg whites, folding and lifting carefully until all is blended lightly.

Slide this into a buttered and floured two-quart soufflé dish and place in a preheated 350° oven for about twenty-five minutes. Test to see if the soufflé is done before removing from the oven.

# Mushroom Soufflé

*Try this with Chicken Breasts in Champagne Sauce (page 128), some Puréed Peas (page 132), and for dessert cut-up fruit with kirsch.*

| | |
|---|---|
| 7 tablespoons butter | 1 cup chicken broth |
| 4 chopped shallots | 4 egg yolks |
| ½ pound fresh mushrooms | 6 egg whites |
| 3 tablespoons flour | ½ teaspoon cream of tartar |

Melt four tablespoons of the butter in a heavy skillet. Peel and chop the shallots and sauté for a minute. Chop fine the mushrooms, both caps and stems, and add to the skillet. Lower the heat. These mushrooms must be cooked very slowly, stirred occasionally. They are finished when all the water has been driven off, about three-quarters of an hour. From this operation you should have about a cup of mushrooms. (Mushrooms prepared in this way are called *duxelles*.)

In the top part of a double boiler (over boiling water) melt the three remaining tablespoons butter. Add the flour. Stir and cook for a few minutes. Pour in the chicken broth and, stirring constantly, cook for about five minutes until the mixture is thick.

Allow this to cool for a few minutes and then beat in the egg yolks. Continue beating until the sauce is smooth.

Stir in the cup of sautéed mushrooms. Then set aside to cool for at least fifteen minutes.

Beat the egg whites into stiff, creamy peaks, sprinkling the cream of tartar over them as you beat. Mix vigorously one-third of the whites into the mushroom sauce. Then dribble this over the remaining egg whites and lift and fold carefully until all is combined.

Slide this into a buttered and floured two-quart soufflé dish.

Bake in a preheated 350° oven for twenty-five minutes. Test for doneness.

## Beef-Broth–Horseradish Soufflé

*As a change from Yorkshire pudding this horseradish soufflé is excellent with roast beef. Add a fresh vegetable, a salad, and a mold of chocolate ice cream, and you have a proper Sunday dinner.*

3 tablespoons butter
3 tablespoons flour
2 cups strong beef bouillon
4 tablespoons grated Parmesan
    cheese

4 egg yolks
2 tablespoons freshly grated
    horseradish
6 egg whites
½ teaspoon cream of tartar

Melt the butter in the top half of a double boiler (over boiling water). Stir in the flour and cook for a few minutes.

Pour in the beef bouillon and add the grated Parmesan cheese. Stir constantly and cook for about five minutes until the mixture is thick and smooth. Remove top part of double boiler from heat.

Allow this mixture to cool and then beat in the egg yolks. Keep beating until all is smooth and creamy. Blend in the freshly grated horseradish.

Beat the egg whites into stiff, moist peaks, sprinkling the cream of tartar over them as you beat.

Combine a third of the beaten whites with the horseradish sauce. Then dribble this over the remaining whites. Lift and fold carefully.

Slide the mixture into a buttered and floured two-quart soufflé dish and place in a preheated 350° oven for twenty-five minutes. Test to make certain the soufflé is done before removing it.

# Dessert Soufflés

Who made the first soufflé? I have not heard. It may easily have been one of the ancients: Roman cooks, if often hysterical with their sauces—garum, for instance—and in their preoccupation with peacocks, were generally competent; one of them could have done it.

We know for certain that in France at the end of the eighteenth century there were soufflés. A vanilla-flavored one was on the menu of a restaurant in Paris called Grande Taverne de Londres, and it was made exactly as a vanilla soufflé is made today.

(You might precede the soufflé with a roast capon, Carrots Vichy, and a watercress salad.)

The instructions follow. . . .

# Vanilla Soufflé

3 tablespoons butter
3 tablespoons flour
1 cup hot milk
½ cup sugar
1 one-inch piece of vanilla bean
   or 1 teaspoon vanilla extract

5 egg yolks
6 egg whites
1 teaspoon cream of tartar

Melt the butter in the top part of a double boiler (over boiling water). Mix in the flour. Cook a minute, add the hot milk, the sugar, and, if you have it, a piece of vanilla bean. If you have no vanilla bean, use vanilla extract, but after the mixture is cooked.

Stir this constantly until it is thick and smooth. Remove from the fire and discard the vanilla bean. (Now add the vanilla extract if that's what you're doing.)

Beat the egg yolks and add to the sauce. Allow the mixture to cool, fifteen minutes at least.

Beat the egg whites until they are stiff and creamy. Sprinkle the cream of tartar over them as you beat.

When the egg whites are stiff add a large spoonful of them to the vanilla mixture, and beat it in thoroughly until the mixture has a slightly foamy texture. Now, dribble all over the remaining egg whites and fold carefully, carefully, until all is mixed thoroughly.

Slide this into a buttered and sugared two-quart soufflé dish and place in a preheated 350° oven.

This should be done in about twenty-five minutes, but test it.

Crushed raspberries, sugared, with a little kirsch, makes a good sauce for this. Or serve with the following:

## SAUCE FOR VANILLA SOUFFLÉ

½ cup orange marmalade      ¼ cup orange juice
½ cup apricot jam           2 teaspoons lemon juice

In the top part of a double boiler (over boiling water) place the orange marmalade and the apricot jam. Cook until they liquefy. Then scrape them into a blender, add the orange juice and lemon juice. Blend until all is smooth.

You can use this sauce either hot or cold.


The vanilla was probably the original dessert soufflé, but you can be sure the French were not satisfied with such simplicity. Also, ovens came into general use in the first part of the nineteenth century, restyling the whole art of cooking, and cooks, taking advantage of the new machine, gave soufflés their fondest attention.

By the time we arrive at the Grande Époque, soufflés have taken on a beaux arts quality. They are complicated, ornate, and extravagant. And they have become a symbol of status. Anyone who was anyone had a soufflé named after him.

Here is what happened to that simple vanilla soufflé when it was served to Brillat-Savarin: The mixture was layered with ladyfingers soaked in rum and dollops of applesauce, and the top was decorated with cherries cooked in syrup.

And Rothschild: The mixture was layered with preserved fruits which had been soaked in Goldvasser and the top decorated with fresh sugared strawberries.

The Tsarina: In the center of the soufflé were placed macaroon pieces soaked in kirsch. As soon as it was taken out of the oven, it was covered with a veil of spun sugar.

Sarah Bernhardt: Her mixture was flavored with macaroon pieces soaked in Curaçao and it was served with large strawberries covered with a purée of more strawberries and more Curaçao, plus a bowl of Chantilly Cream.

## Grand Marnier Soufflé

*You should have something gala before this, say a crown roast of lamb whose center you have filled with sautéed mushrooms, and a salad of Belgian endive on which you have placed a slice of pâté de foie gras.*

| | |
|---|---|
| 3 tablespoons butter | 5 egg yolks |
| 2 tablespoons flour | 5 tablespoons Grand Marnier |
| 1 cup heavy cream | ½ teaspoon cream of tartar |
| 6 tablespoons sugar | 6 egg whites |

In the top part of a double boiler (over boiling water) melt the butter and add the flour. Mix well and cook for a moment. Then pour in the cream, stir constantly until this thickens, and then add the sugar. When the sugar has dissolved, remove top part of double boiler from the heat, and allow to cool.

When the mixture is cool, beat the egg yolks and stir them into it along with the Grand Marnier.

Sprinkle the cream of tartar over the egg whites while you beat them into stiff, moist peaks. Take a third of the beaten whites and mix vigorously into the Grand Marnier sauce. Pour gently over the remaining whites and lift and fold to combine.

Slide the soufflé mixture into a buttered and sugared dish and place in a preheated 350° oven for about twenty minutes. Test to make certain the soufflé is done before removing from the oven.

# Coffee Soufflé

*Here is something to top off an economical dinner. Have a well-marinated flank steak, Potatoes Anna (page 133), and fresh-cooked spinach dressed with oil and vinegar.*

| | |
|---|---|
| 3 tablespoons butter | ½ cup sugar |
| 3 tablespoons flour | 4 egg yolks |
| ½ cup hot milk | 5 egg whites |
| ½ cup strong black coffee | ½ teaspoon cream of tartar |

Melt the butter in the top part of a double boiler and mix in the flour. Cook a minute. Add the hot milk and the coffee. Add the sugar and cook and stir constantly until the mixture is well combined. Set top part of double boiler off the fire.

Beat the egg yolks and when the mixture is slightly cool, add them to it.

Beat the egg whites until stiff, sprinkling the cream of tartar over them as you beat. When the mixture is really cool, add a large spoonful of the whites and combine thoroughly with it, then add this to the remaining egg whites, and fold and fold, gently.

Pour this into a buttered and sugared two-quart soufflé dish and place in a preheated 350° oven. This should take about twenty-five minutes, but test it.

The best sauce for this coffee soufflé is simply whipped cream, thoroughly chilled, with a little brandy added.

# Lemon Soufflé

*For this and the Orange Soufflé which follows here is a possible dinner: mixed seafoods in a mild curry sauce, herbed rice, a salad of Boston lettuce with oil and vinegar dressing.*

| | |
|---|---|
| 3 tablespoons butter | ½ cup sugar |
| 3 tablespoons flour | 2 lemons |
| 1 cup light cream | 5 egg whites |
| 4 egg yolks | ½ teaspoon cream of tartar |

In the top part of the double boiler (over boiling water) melt the butter and mix in the flour. Cook a minute. Then add the light cream. Stir this—and it won't take long—until it is thick and smooth. Take top part of double boiler off the heat to cool.

Beat the egg yolks with a scant half cup sugar, add to the sauce, and beat all together.

Take a large, fresh lemon and grate fine all of its rind into a bowl. Add the juice from that lemon and one other.

Beat the egg whites till they are stiff and glistening, sprinkling the cream of tartar over them as you beat. When egg-cream mixture is cool, add the lemon juice and rind; beat well.

Take a large spoonful of the whites and mix well into the lemon sauce until it appears slightly foamy. Dribble the sauce over the remaining egg whites and lift and fold gently and thoroughly.

Slide this mixture into a buttered and sugared two-quart soufflé dish and place in a preheated 350° oven. This should be done in twenty-five minutes, but test it. Serve with:

## FRESH STRAWBERRY SAUCE

Cut up two cups of fresh strawberries, large ones in quarters, small ones in halves. Beat two or three tablespoons red currant jelly and pour over the berries with a sprinkle of kirsch. Put this in the icebox for a couple of hours to get very cold.


## Orange Soufflé

| | |
|---|---|
| 3 tablespoons butter | ½ cup sugar |
| 3 tablespoons flour | 1 orange |
| 1 cup heavy cream | 5 egg whites |
| 4 egg yolks | ½ teaspoon cream of tartar |

In the top part of a double boiler (over boiling water) melt the butter; mix in three tablespoons flour. Cook a minute. Then add the cream. Stir this—and it won't take long—until it is thick and smooth. Take the top part of double boiler off the heat to cool.

Beat the egg yolks with a scant half cup of sugar. Add to the sauce and beat all together.

Take a large, fresh orange and grate fine all of its rind into a bowl. Use the juice of the orange, to make one half cup.

Beat the egg whites till they are stiff and glistening, sprinkling the cream of tartar over them as you beat. When the egg-cream mixture is cool, add the orange juice and the orange rind; beat well.

Take a large spoonful of the whites and mix well into the orange sauce until it appears slightly foamy. Dribble the sauce over the remaining egg whites and lift and fold gently and thoroughly.

Slide this mixture into a buttered and sugared two-quart soufflé dish and place in a preheated 350° oven. This should be done in twenty-five minutes, but test it.

Use the same strawberry sauce as for Lemon Soufflé.

# Banana Soufflé

*To begin with have two small roasting chickens stuffed with wild rice and basted with red currant jelly, and braised fresh celery.*

| | |
|---|---|
| 1 cup milk | 3 tablespoons flour |
| 3 bananas | 5 egg yolks |
| Sugar | 6 egg whites |
| ½ cup water | ½ teaspoon cream of tartar |
| 1 tablespoon minced chutney | |
| 3 tablespoons butter | |

Put the milk and one banana in a blender and run until smooth. Slice the remaining two bananas.

Make a sugar syrup by boiling together the two tablespoons sugar, the water, and the minced chutney. When this mixture has boiled down and become syrupy poach the banana slices in it for a few minutes until they begin to soften. Then pour all of this—bananas, chutney, syrup—into the bottom of a buttered two-quart soufflé dish. Keep warm.

In the top part of the double boiler (over boiling water) melt the butter; mix in the flour. Cook a minute. Then add the cup of banana-milk from the blender. Stir this—and it won't take long—until it is thick and smooth. Take the top part of the double boiler off the heat and cool.

Beat the egg yolks with a scant half cup of sugar. Add to the sauce and beat all together.

Beat the egg whites till they are stiff and glistening, sprinkling the cream of tartar over them as you beat.

Take a large spoonful of the whites and mix well into the banana sauce until it appears slightly foamy. Dribble the sauce over the remaining egg whites and lift and fold gently and thoroughly.

Slide this mixture into the soufflé dish on top of the sliced bananas and place in a preheated 350° oven.

This should be done in about twenty-five minutes, but test it.

*For the two soufflés that follow you might well start off with cold lobster mayonnaise, and asparagus with drawn butter.*

## Strawberry Soufflé

FOR THE MARINADE:

2 cups sliced strawberries

½ cup orange juice

1 teaspoon lemon juice

3 tablespoons Cointreau

1 tablespoon sugar

FOR THE SOUFFLÉ:

3 tablespoons butter

3 tablespoons flour

½ cup marinade

1 teaspoon grated lemon rind

½ cup sugar

¾ cup milk

4 egg yolks

6 egg whites

½ teaspoon cream of tartar

Pour over the sliced strawberries the orange juice, lemon juice, Cointreau, and sugar. Let this steep for at least an hour.

Melt the butter in the top part of a double boiler (over boiling water). Blend in the flour and cook for a minute or two. Add one-half cup of the drained marinade, the grated lemon rind, sugar, and milk. Stir constantly and cook until all is blended into a smooth sauce. This should take about five minutes.

Remove the top part of the double boiler from the heat. Allow to cool for a few minutes and then beat in the egg yolks. Beat the mixture until it is smooth and creamy. Allow it to cool for at least fifteen minutes.

Beat the egg whites, sprinkling the cream of tartar as you beat.

Spoon about a third of the whites into the cooled mixture and combine vigorously. Then dribble this over the remaining egg whites. Lift and fold carefully until all is combined.

Heat the sliced, drained strawberries and place in the bottom of a buttered and sugared two-quart soufflé dish. Pour the soufflé mixture over them. Place in a preheated 350° oven and bake for about twenty-five minutes. Test to see if done.

## Strawberry-Raspberry Soufflé

| | |
|---|---|
| 2 cups sliced ripe strawberries | 4 egg yolks, beaten |
| Sugar | 1 cup raspberry purée (fresh |
| 2 tablespoons red currant jelly | or frozen) |
| 3 tablespoons butter | 5 egg whites |
| 3 tablespoons flour | ½ teaspoon cream of tartar |
| ½ cup milk | |

In a dish place the strawberries, sprinkle with a little sugar, and pour over them the currant jelly, which you have beaten with a fork.

In the top part of a double boiler (over boiling water) melt the butter and stir in the flour. Cook for a few minutes, then stir in the milk. Cook for about five minutes, stirring constantly, until all is blended into a smooth sauce.

Remove the top part of the double boiler from heat and allow to cool for a while. Then add the beaten egg yolks. Stir until the mixture is smooth.

Add the puréed raspberries. Sweeten with one tablespoon sugar, if necessary. Set aside to cool for about fifteen minutes.

Beat the egg whites. Sprinkle in the cream of tartar while beating the whites into stiff, creamy peaks.

After the raspberry sauce has cooled, spoon in a third of the egg whites. Combine vigorously. Then dribble the sauce over the remaining whites. Lift and fold carefully until all is gently blended.

Heat the sliced strawberries and place in the bottom of a buttered and sugared two-quart soufflé dish. Pour the raspberry sauce over them.

Bake in a preheated 350° oven for about twenty-five minutes. Test for doneness before removing from the oven.

# Apple Soufflé

*Bake a good fish—striped bass, Spanish mackerel, red snapper—
in butter and dry vermouth and surround it with little red boiled
potatoes. Add a platter of broccoli with Hollandaise sauce.*

FOR THE SYRUP:
½ cup sugar
½ cup water
1 teaspoon lemon juice

FOR THE SOUFFLÉ:
4 medium-size tart green
   apples
3 tablespoons butter

3 tablespoons flour
1½ cups apple juice or sweet
   cider
4 tablespoons sugar
4 egg yolks
6 egg whites
½ teaspoon cream of tartar
¾ cup crumbled macaroons
1 teaspoon apple brandy

Make a sugar syrup of the sugar, water, and lemon juice.

Peel, core, and slice the apples rather thin. Poach the slices for
a few minutes in the syrup—you will have to do a few at a time.
As you take the slices out of the syrup—with a slotted spoon—
place them in the bottom of a buttered and sugared two-quart
soufflé dish. Keep warm.

Melt the butter in the top part of a double boiler (over boiling
water). Add the flour and cook for a few minutes. Pour in the
apple juice and sugar. Stir constantly and cook for five minutes
or so until the mixture is thick and smooth. Remove from the
heat.

Beat the egg yolks and stir into mixture. Beat until this is
smooth. Allow to cool for fifteen minutes or longer.

Beat the egg whites into stiff, moist peaks. Sprinkle the cream
of tartar over the whites as you beat them. Spoon a third of these

over the apple-juice mixture and combine vigorously. Dribble this foamy sauce over the remaining egg whites and lift and fold carefully until all is combined.

Sprinkle the crumbled macaroons with the apple brandy. Spoon nine-tenths of the batter over the poached apple slices, then sprinkle the macaroons on top and finish with the last few spoonfuls of the soufflé batter. Bake in a preheated 350° oven for about twenty-five minutes. But test.

## Ginger Soufflé

*With this soufflé let us have a Stuffed Leg of Young Veal (page 129), stuffed with prosciutto and mushrooms, cooked on a bed of tiny buttered white onions and basted with Chablis, and a salad of Young Lettuce (page 70) in a light cream and lemon juice dressing.*

FOR THE POACHING SYRUP:
2 tablespoons apple brandy
2 tablespoons chopped crystallized ginger
1 teaspoon lemon juice
2 tablespoons sugar
2 tablespoons water

FOR THE SOUFFLÉ:
4 medium-size tart green apples
½ cup powdered ginger snaps
3 tablespoons butter
1½ cups sweet cider
4 tablespoons sugar
2 egg yolks
6 egg whites
½ teaspoon cream of tartar

Peel, core, and slice the apples moderately thin. Make a syrup with the above ingredients and poach the apple slices in it for a few minutes, until softened.

When you have finished, take out the ginger and put it with the apples and two or three tablespoons of the syrup in the bottom of a buttered and sugared two-quart soufflé dish. Keep warm.

Place very crisp ginger snaps in the blender and run until they are reduced to a powder.

Melt the butter in the top part of a double boiler (over boiling water). Stir in the powdered ginger snaps. Cook for a few minutes, then pour in the cider and sugar. Stir constantly and cook for about five minutes until the mixture is smooth and thick.

Remove from the heat and cool for a moment. Beat the egg yolks into the mixture. Then set it aside to cool for at least fifteen minutes.

Beat the egg whites into stiff, creamy peaks. Sprinkle cream of tartar over them as you beat. Spoon a third of the whites into the ginger-snap sauce and combine vigorously. Dribble this over the remaining beaten whites and lift and fold carefully until all combines lightly.

Pour this sauce over the warm apple slices in the soufflé dish.

Bake in a preheated oven of 350°. This should be done in about twenty-five minutes, but test it.

Here following is a burst of chocolate soufflés. They seem to me to be the best of all dessert soufflés.

And here is a dinner which will suit any one of them:

Caviar Mousse
A Whole Beef Fillet Larded with Foie Gras
Artichoke Bottoms Stuffed with Puréed Lettuce
Green Salad

# Chocolate Soufflé

3 tablespoons butter
3 tablespoons flour
1 cup hot milk
½ cup sugar
1½ squares bitter cooking
  chocolate, grated

Dash of salt
5 egg yolks
7 egg whites
½ teaspoon cream of tartar

In the top part of a double boiler (over boiling water) melt the butter and mix in the flour. Cook a moment. Then add the hot milk, and stir constantly until the mixture is thick and creamy.

Add the sugar. Stir until dissolved. Add the chocolate.

The mixture will appear grainy for a while but, as you keep stirring, suddenly the chocolate will combine and you will have a smooth, thick, elegant sauce.

Take this off the fire. Add a dash of salt and beat the mixture for a minute. Allow it to cool a bit, then add the beaten egg yolks to it, and beat until smooth.

Beat the egg whites until stiff. Sprinkle the cream of tartar over them as you beat. When the sauce is really cool, take a large spoonful of the egg whites and fold vigorously into the chocolate mixture until it appears slightly foamy. Then dribble this sauce over the remaining egg whites and fold thoroughly and carefully.

Slide all this into a buttered and sugared two-quart soufflé dish and place in a preheated 350° oven for about twenty-five minutes.

Here's a fine simple, perfect sauce:

## VANILLA ICE CREAM SAUCE

Beat a half pint heavy cream until it's stiff. Allow a half pint vanilla ice cream to soften—not melt, soften. Then beat these two together. Add a couple of tablespoons good brandy.

# Chocolate Grand Marnier Soufflé

3 tablespoons butter

3 tablespoons flour

1 cup hot milk

½ cup sugar

1 square bitter cooking chocolate, grated

4 tablespoons Grand Marnier

Dash of salt

5 egg yolks

7 egg whites

½ teaspoon cream of tartar

¼ cup candied orange peel, chopped

Melt the butter in the top part of a double boiler over boiling water. Mix in the flour. Cook for a moment. Add the hot milk and stir constantly until the mixture is thick and creamy.

Stir in the sugar. When this dissolves, add the grated chocolate. Keep stirring until the grainy mixture smooths to a rich, thick sauce.

Remove the top part of the double boiler from flame. Add the Grand Marnier and a dash of salt. Beat this for a minute, then allow to cool for a while. Add the beaten egg yolks to the mixture and beat until smooth.

Beat the egg whites until stiff. Sprinkle the cream of tartar over them as you beat. Take one large spoonful of the whites and stir vigorously into the chocolate sauce until it appears slightly foamy. Then dribble the sauce over the remaining egg whites and fold thoroughly and carefully.

Slide the mixture into a buttered and sugared two-quart soufflé dish. Place in a preheated 350° oven and bake for about twenty-five minutes. Test to see if done.

Sprinkle top of soufflé with the chopped candied orange peel.

# Chocolate Soufflé with Pecans

3 tablespoons butter
3 tablespoons flour
1 cup hot milk
½ cup sugar
1½ squares bitter cooking chocolate, grated
Dash of salt

5 egg yolks, beaten
½ cup broken-up pecans (if you'd prefer hazelnuts, use them or slivered almonds or walnut meats)
7 egg whites
½ teaspoon cream of tartar

In the top part of a double boiler (over boiling water) melt the butter, and stir in the flour. Cook for a moment. Add the hot milk and cook, stirring constantly, until the mixture is thick and creamy.

Add the sugar and stir until dissolved. Then add the grated chocolate. Keep stirring until the chocolate combines to form a thick, smooth, elegant sauce.

Take mixture off the fire and add a dash of salt. Beat the sauce for about a minute. Allow it to cool somewhat and then add the beaten egg yolks to it. Beat mixture until smooth, adding in the pecans.

Beat the egg whites until stiff. Sprinkle the cream of tartar over them as you beat. When the sauce is really cool, take a large spoonful of the egg whites and fold vigorously into the sauce until it appears slightly foamy. Then dribble the sauce over the remaining egg whites and fold thoroughly and carefully.

Slide this mixture into a buttered and sugared two-quart soufflé dish. Place in a preheated 350° oven, and bake for about twenty-five minutes. But, of course, test it.

# Chocolate-Mocha Soufflé

3 tablespoons butter
3 tablespoons flour
1 cup hot milk
½ cup sugar
1 tablespoon instant coffee
1½ squares bitter cooking
   chocolate, grated

Dash of salt
½ cup candy coffee beans
5 egg yolks, beaten
7 egg whites
½ teaspoon cream of tartar

In the top part of a double boiler (over boiling water) melt the butter. Stir in the flour. Cook a moment. Then add the hot milk and stir constantly until the mixture is thick and smooth.

Add the sugar and instant coffee. Stir mixture until these ingredients dissolve. Then add the grated chocolate. This will take a while to combine, but keep stirring and suddenly you will have a rich, smooth sauce.

Take from the fire and add a dash of salt and the candy coffee beans. Beat for a moment. Allow the mixture to cool a bit and then add the beaten egg yolks to it. Beat until smooth.

Beat the egg whites until stiff and sprinkle the cream of tartar over them as you beat. When the sauce has cooled to room temperature, take a large spoonful of the whites and fold vigorously into the chocolate-mocha mixture until it appears slightly foamy. Dribble this sauce over the remaining egg whites and fold carefully and thoroughly.

Slide the sauce into a buttered and sugared two-quart soufflé dish. Place in a preheated 350° oven and bake for about twenty-five minutes. Test to be certain it is done.

# Chocolate Soufflé with Candied Cherries

3 tablespoons butter
3 tablespoons flour
1 cup hot milk
½ cup sugar
1 square bitter cooking chocolate, grated

5 tablespoons Cherry Heering
Dash of salt
5 egg yolks, beaten
1 dozen or so candied cherries
7 egg whites
½ teaspoon cream of tartar

Melt the butter in the top part of a double boiler (over boiling water). Mix in the flour. Cook a moment and then add the hot milk. Stir constantly until the mixture is rich and creamy.

Add the sugar. Stir until this dissolves and then add the grated chocolate.

Keep stirring until the mixture ceases to appear grainy and becomes a smooth, thick sauce. At that point, take it off the flame and add four tablespoons of the Cherry Heering to it. Also add a dash of salt. Beat this mixture for a moment. After it has cooled a bit, add the beaten egg yolks and beat until smooth.

While this cools completely, butter and sugar a two-quart soufflé dish and line the bottom with the candied cherries. Sprinkle these with the remaining tablespoon Cherry Heering. Preheat the oven to 350°.

Then beat the egg whites until stiff, sprinkling the cream of tartar over them as you beat. Fold vigorously one large spoonful of the whites into the sauce until it appears slightly foamy. Dribble this mixture over the remaining egg whites and fold carefully, thoroughly.

Slide this into the soufflé dish and cook for about twenty-five minutes.

# Chocolate-Mint Soufflé

3 tablespoons butter
3 tablespoons flour
1 cup hot milk
½ cup sugar
1 square bitter cooking chocolate, grated

4 tablespoons green crème de menthe liqueur
Dash of salt
5 egg yolks, beaten
7 egg whites
½ teaspoon cream of tartar

In the top part of a double boiler (over boiling water) melt the butter and mix in the flour. Cook a moment, then add the hot milk. Stir constantly until the mixture is thick and creamy.

Add the sugar and stir until dissolved. Then add the grated chocolate. The mixture will appear grainy for a while but, as you keep stirring, suddenly the chocolate will combine and you will have a smooth, thick, elegant sauce.

Take the top part of the double boiler off the fire and add the crème de menthe and a dash of salt. Beat the mixture for a minute. Allow it to cool a bit, then add the beaten egg yolks to it and beat until smooth.

Beat the egg whites until stiff and sprinkle the cream of tartar over them as you beat. When the sauce is really cool, take a large spoonful of the egg whites and fold vigorously into the chocolate-mint mixture until it appears slightly foamy. Then dribble this sauce over the remaining egg whites and fold thoroughly and carefully.

Slide the mixture into a buttered and sugared two-quart soufflé dish and place in a preheated 350° oven.

The soufflé should be done in about twenty-five minutes, but test it.

# Chocolate Soufflé with Brandied Macaroons

½ cup macaroons crumbled
2 tablespoons brandy
3 tablespoons butter
3 tablespoons flour
1 cup hot milk
½ cup sugar

1 square bitter cooking chocolate, grated
Dash of salt
5 egg yolks
7 egg whites
½ teaspoon cream of tartar

Crumble the macaroons and sprinkle with the brandy. Set aside.

In the top half of a double boiler (over boiling water) melt the butter, then mix in the flour. Cook for a moment and then add the hot milk. Stir constantly until you have a thick and creamy mixture.

Stir in the sugar. After it dissolves, mix in the grated chocolate. Stir constantly until the chocolate blends completely into a smooth sauce.

Take the top part of double boiler from the heat and add a dash of salt. Beat for a moment and then allow to cool for a minute or two. Beat the egg yolks and add to mixture, continuing beating until mixture is smooth.

Beat the egg whites until stiff, sprinkling the cream of tartar over them as you beat. Take one large spoonful of these whites and stir vigorously into the chocolate sauce until it appears somewhat foamy. Dribble this mixture over the remaining whites and then fold carefully and thoroughly.

Slip this into a buttered and sugared two-quart soufflé dish, place in a preheated 350° oven, and bake for approximately twenty-five minutes.

When soufflé appears done, strew brandied macaroon crumbles across the top.

# Triple Vanilla Chocolate Soufflé

3 tablespoons butter
3 tablespoons flour
1 cup hot milk
½-pound bar Maillard's triple vanilla chocolate

Dash of salt
5 egg yolks, beaten
7 egg whites
½ teaspoon cream of tartar

In the top half of a double boiler (over boiling water) melt the butter. Mix in the flour and cook for a moment. Add the hot milk and stir constantly until the mixture is rich and creamy.

Break up the triple vanilla chocolate and add to mixture. Stir until all blend into a thick, smooth sauce.

Take the top part of double boiler off fire, add a dash of salt, and beat for a minute. Allow the mixture to cool a bit and then add the beaten egg yolks to it. Beat mixture until smooth.

Beat the egg whites until stiff. Sprinkle the cream of tartar over them as you beat. When the sauce is really cool, fold in vigorously one large spoonful of the egg whites. When the mixture appears slightly foamy, dribble it over the remaining egg whites and fold thoroughly and carefully.

Slide all this into a buttered and sugared two-quart soufflé dish and place in a preheated 350° oven for about twenty-five minutes. Test to make certain soufflé is done before removing from oven.

# Chocolate Soufflé with Liqueur-Filled Chocolates

3 tablespoons butter
3 tablespoons flour
1 cup hot milk
½ cup sugar
1 square bitter cooking chocolate, grated
Dash of salt

5 egg yolks, beaten
7 egg whites
½ teaspoon cream of tartar
1 dozen or so liqueur-filled chocolates (cognac, Grand Marnier, kümmel, etc.)

Melt the butter in the top part of a double boiler (over boiling water). Stir in the flour and cook for a moment. Add the hot milk. Stir mixture constantly until it is thick and creamy.

Add the sugar and stir until it is dissolved. Then add the grated chocolate. The mixture will appear grainy for a while but, as you keep stirring, suddenly the chocolate will combine and the sauce will become thick, smooth, and elegant.

Remove the top part of double boiler from fire and add a dash of salt. Beat the mixture for a minute, then allow it to cool a bit.

Add the beaten egg yolks to the sauce and beat until smooth.

Beat the egg whites until stiff, sprinkling the cream of tartar over them as you beat. When the sauce is really cool, fold vigorously a large spoonful of the whites into the mixture. It should appear slightly foamy. Then dribble this over the remaining egg whites and fold thoroughly and carefully.

Slide five-sixths of this into a buttered and sugared two-quart soufflé dish. Then lay the liqueur-filled chocolates on top. Spoon the remaining sixth of the soufflé sauce over the chocolates.

Bake in a preheated 350° oven for about twenty-five minutes. But test it.

# The Simplest Chocolate Soufflé

3 tablespoons butter
3 tablespoons flour
1 cup hot milk
¾ cup bottled or canned sweet chocolate syrup

Dash of salt
5 egg yolks, beaten
7 egg whites
¾ teaspoon cream of tartar

In the top part of a double boiler (over boiling water) melt the butter and mix in the flour. Cook a moment. Then add the hot milk. Stir constantly until the mixture is thick and creamy.

Add the chocolate syrup. Stir until sauce is smooth and thick.

Remove the top part of double boiler from fire. Add a dash of salt and beat the mixture for a minute. Allow to cool, then add the beaten egg yolks and beat mixture until smooth.

Beat the egg whites until stiff and sprinkle the cream of tartar over them as you beat. When the sauce is really cool, take a large spoonful of the stiff egg whites and stir vigorously into the mixture until it appears slightly foamy. Dribble this over the remaining egg whites, folding thoroughly and carefully.

Slide all this into a buttered and sugared two-quart soufflé dish and place in a preheated 350° oven.

This should be done in about twenty-five minutes, but test it.

# Quiches

"Quiche," says the Oxford French Dictionary, "is a sort of thick custard, specialty of Lorraine."

And indeed in the beginning it was just that, a thick custard made with eight egg yolks, a pint of cream, and a pinch of nutmeg. Bathers in the chilly lakes of the Vosges mountains liked to eat a slice as they were drying off.

The first variation I find in Escoffier. He says that the crust was covered with slices of lean cooked bacon, then the custard poured over that. He also says that the bacon may be mingled with thin slices of Gruyère cheese, but—and he points his admonitory finger—"This is contrary to local custom."

What kind of shaking finger would that purist point now? We, epigonous meddlers, have had at the quiche to a point where Lorraine quakes. Anything goes. Lobsters, cauliflower, anchovies, mushrooms—whatever is good is proper.

So now, a quiche is a custard baked in a crust, flavored with whatever. The goodness of it depends on the crispness of the crust, for the fillings are no problem at all.

Therefore, a word about crusts:

If you are a great pastry maker, and know exactly what you are doing, follow your bent.

But, if you are not, and would like to know the way to make a rich and easy crust, here is one that was first written down by Sir Kenelm Digby three hundred years ago:

In a bowl place three ounces (a small package) of cream cheese, add to it three ounces of soft butter (that's three-quarters of a stick), mash them together with a wooden spoon until they are completely combined, sprinkle over this three-quarters of a cup of flour and a dash of salt, then with a silver fork mash and mix the mass until you have a bowl full of tiny grains. You can pick this up now and by kneading only once or twice you will have a cohesive mass.

Put this in the refrigerator under a sheet of wax paper until it is very cold—some say overnight but actually three or four hours is enough.

An hour before you are ready to use the dough, take it out and roll it between two pieces of wax paper. It will make exactly enough for an eight-inch pie pan.

Fit it into the pan, crimp the edges, cover it again, and place it in the freezing compartment of the refrigerator. It *must* stay in the freezer for at least three-quarters of an hour. Then take it out, jab it all over with the tines of a fork, and place it in a preheated 400-degree oven. Let it stay there for six to seven minutes, or until it has just begun to color; then take it out and it is ready to be filled.

I suspect, however, that rather than bothering with the above what you will do is buy a ready-made pie shell. Surprisingly, there are some very good ones. Small baking companies all over the country are making them—and with real butter. You will find them in the frozen-food compartments in many markets; just be sure you get a good one.

The procedure with one of these is this: Remove the shell from your own freezing compartment, jab it all over with the tines of a fork, and place it immediately in a preheated 400° oven for six or seven minutes. Then it is ready to be used.

If you cannot eat a quiche in traditional style—beside a cool mountain lake—but must sit at a table indoors, you will probably want to pretend that you are having a proper meal, and so must have accompaniments.

But a quiche is so rich—cream, eggs, crust—that all you need is a salad and an ending.

The cliché endings are the best—a water ice or a piece of fruit.

You might try for a little more variety in the salad. The first impulse, at the thought of salad, is to buy whatever lettuce is freshest in the market, then wash it, roll it up in a towel, and refrigerate. But occasionally it's good to have something a little different. So try:

## Carrot Salad

Cut a half-dozen fair-sized carrots in julienne strips—let's hope you have a machine that does it for you. Cook the strips in salted water for a few minutes until they just begin to soften, then drain them and chill well in the refrigerator.

Make an ordinary French dressing—4 parts oil, 1 part vinegar, salt, and pepper—and marinate the carrots in this for an hour before serving.

# Cucumber Salad

Peel and slice very thin two medium cucumbers. Sprinkle the slices with salt—quite a lot of salt—and let stand for a couple of hours. Then drain and rinse them, pat dry, cover with a French dressing (as above), and chill well in the refrigerator.

# Young Lettuce Salad

This is really best with early lettuce out of your own garden. Wash and refrigerate, then just before serving mix it with this dressing: Three parts light cream, one part lemon juice or white vinegar, salt, and pepper.

# Celery Root Salad

Peel three medium celery roots and cut them into julienne strips (hopefully with that machine) and immediately plunge them into ice water. (They turn brown if you don't.) Make a cup of fresh mayonnaise in your blender but add a level teaspoon dry mustard to the usual formula. Dry the celery root and mix with the dressing just before serving.

# Pepper Salad

Buy three sweet peppers—a red, a yellow, a green. Core and seed them and then slice in whole rings. Add several slices of onion rings. Serve with a French dressing.

## Belgian Endive Salad

Slice each endive in four lengthwise; chill well. Have on the table a bowl of coarse salt. Eat the endive with your fingers, and salt them as you please.

## Tomato Salad

This is only possible for a few weeks of the year when you can get local field-grown tomatoes. Peel them, slice thin, spread them out on a platter, sprinkle them with chopped dill, and then pour over them the usual French dressing. Let stand in the refrigerator for at least an hour.

## String Bean Salad

This sounds frightful but is actually very good. Buy an ordinary can of whole green string beans and one of yellow wax beans. Drain them, put them in a bowl. Core and seed a sweet red pepper, mince it very fine and add to the beans. Now make this peculiar dressing: a half cup vinegar, a sixth cup oil, salt, and pepper, plus a quarter cup sugar. Pour this over the beans and let them marinate in it for at least twenty-four hours. Forty-eight is better.

## Watercress Salad

Wash and cut off all the stems of a couple of bunches of watercress. Dry, refrigerate, and just before serving mix with ordinary French dressing. Nothing could be simpler or better.

## Pickled Beets

Buy a jar of sliced pickled beets, put them in a bowl with their marinade and grate half a sweet onion over them.

## Fresh Mushroom Salad

Use the caps only of a pound of fresh white mushrooms. Slice the mushrooms horizontally very thin. Put them in a bowl and sprinkle over them a handful of chopped fresh parsley. Make a dressing of four parts olive oil, one part lemon juice, salt, and pepper. Mix just before serving.

## Cauliflower Salad

Pull apart a head of cauliflower into bite-size flowerets. Plunge these into boiling, slightly salted water and cook for no more than four minutes. Drain, refrigerate, and mix with French dressing about a half hour before serving.

# Quiche Lorraine

3  small eggs
1  cup heavy cream
A dash of salt
1  cup grated Gruyère cheese
1  eight-inch pie crust ready for
   use

8  strips bacon, cooked and
   crumbled
1  tablespoon butter

In a bowl beat the eggs with a whisk, add the cream and beat again, and add a dash of salt. Sprinkle the cheese in the bottom of the crust; do the same with the bacon; then pour over it the cream and eggs. Cut the butter into small hunks and dot the top of the quiche with it.

Put the pan on a cookie sheet and slip it carefully—you hope it won't spill—into a preheated 350° oven.

Classically, it will be done in forty minutes, but it may take a little less. The quiche is ready when it is puffed up into a dome and slightly browned. Take it out then, slide it off the cookie tin, and wait for at least half an hour before eating. The puffiness will subside, but don't let that alarm you; this is not a soufflé. The correct temperature at which to eat it is pleasantly warm.

# Alsatian Quiche

3 small eggs
1 cup heavy cream
½ cup sweet onion, grated
8 strips bacon, cooked and
  crumbled

1 eight-inch pie crust ready for
  use
¾ cup freshly grated Parmesan cheese
1 tablespoon butter

In a bowl beat the eggs with a whisk, add the cream and beat again, add the grated onion and beat yet again.

Sprinkle the bacon in the bottom of the shell, with the Parmesan over it, then pour over the cream mixture. Dot the top with bits of butter.

Place the pan on a cookie sheet and slide into a preheated 350° oven. It will take about forty minutes to bake. Cool for at least half an hour before serving. (You can of course vary the above recipe: using just bacon and onion, or just cheese and onion.)

NOTE: The Alsatians, if you listen to them, claim also to have invented the quiche, and who knows, they are right next door to Lorraine. The phenomenon may have occurred in the two places simultaneously. The difference between them is this: the Alsatians almost always include onions in their quiche.

# Crab Quiche

3 small eggs
1 cup heavy cream
Dash of salt
1 eight-inch pie crust ready for
  use

1 cup fresh crabmeat
¾ cup grated Gruyère
1 tablespoon butter

In a bowl beat the eggs with a whisk, add the cream, beat again, and add a dash of salt.

In the bottom of the crust lay the crabmeat, which you have picked over well to remove bits of cartilage. Cover crabmeat with the cheese, then pour over the cream mixture. Dot with the butter, put the pie on a cookie sheet, and slide into a 350° oven to bake for forty minutes. Cool for at least half an hour before serving.

## Lobster Quiche

| | |
|---|---|
| ½ cup celery, minced | 1 cup heavy cream |
| 1 cup cooked lobster meat, coarsely chopped | Dash of salt |
| ¼ cup sherry | 1 eight-inch pie crust ready for use |
| 3 small eggs | 1 tablespoon butter |

Boil the celery in a little water for seven or eight minutes, or until it is just beginning to soften. Drain it, place it in a bowl with the lobster, pour over this the sherry, stir, and allow these ingredients to commune with each other for a half hour or so.

Now, in a bowl, beat the eggs, add the cream and the salt, beat again. Arrange the lobster-celery mixture in the bottom of the crust, pour over it the cream mixture, dot with butter.

Place the pan on a cookie sheet and slide into a preheated 350° oven. It will take about forty minutes to bake. Allow to cool for at least thirty minutes before serving.

# Quiche DuBarry

1 small head cauliflower
3 small eggs
1 cup heavy cream
1 cup grated Gruyère cheese
1 eight-inch pie crust

2 tablespoons Parmesan
cheese, freshly grated
1 tablespoon butter

Now, first, place the cauliflower, head down, in a pan of boiling water. Cook until it just begins to be tender, ten or twelve minutes. Remove from the pot, cool, and cut into small flowerets.

Beat the eggs, add the cream, beat again.

Place the Gruyère cheese in the bottom of the crust, cover it with the cream-egg mixture, then dot the top with the cauliflower flowerets (generously). Push them down a bit to be sure they are covered with the cream. They will pop back up again, and when they do, sprinkle the Parmesan over them.

Dot the quiche with butter, put the pan on a cookie sheet and place in 350° oven. Cook for forty minutes or until done. Cool for at least half an hour before serving.


# Quiche with Tuna Fish and Mushrooms

1 cup thinly sliced fresh mushroom caps
Butter
1 small can tuna fish

3 small eggs
1 cup heavy cream
1 ready-to-use eight-inch pie
crust

Sauté the mushrooms gently in a little butter until they just begin to soften. Then add the tuna fish, well drained, and separate it lightly with a fork.

Beat the eggs, add the cream, and beat again.

Place the mushroom-tuna mixture in the bottom of the crust, add the cream mixture, dot with one tablespoon butter.

Place on a cookie sheet in a 350° oven and bake for forty minutes or until done. Cool for at least thirty minutes and serve.

## Quiche with Puréed Chestnuts

| | |
|---|---|
| 1 cup chestnut purée | 3 small eggs |
| Heavy cream | 1 ready-to-use eight-inch pie |
| Butter | crust |
| Salt | |

You can buy unsweetened chestnut purée—it comes in a can from France naturally. When you take it out of the can it is very stiff. Scoop out a cup of it, place it in the top part of a double boiler over boiling water, add a little cream and a couple of teaspoons butter, heat, and mash with a wooden spoon until you have a smooth purée. Add salt rather generously, but taste before you become too generous; the salt, you will find, brings out the taste of the chestnuts.

Beat the eggs, add one cup cream and beat again.

Then pour the chestnut purée into the pie crust. Add the cream mixture, dot with about one tablespoon butter, and place the pan on a cookie sheet in a 350° oven. Bake for forty minutes or until done. Cool for at least a half hour before serving.

# Quiche with Anchovies and Black Olives

3 small eggs
1 cup heavy cream
2 tablespoons anchovy paste
1 cup thinly sliced black olives

1 eight-inch pie crust ready for use
1 tablespoon butter

Beat the eggs with a whisk, add the cream, and beat again. Add the anchovy paste; beat again.

Scatter the sliced olives over the bottom of the crust, pour over it the cream mixture, and dot with butter.

Slide on a cookie sheet into a 350° oven and bake for forty minutes. Cool for at least thirty minutes before serving.

# Quiche with Duxelles and Bacon

¾ pound fresh mushrooms
1 shallot
Butter
8 strips bacon, cooked

3 small eggs
1 cup heavy cream
1 eight-inch pie crust ready for use

First, make duxelles. Chop the mushrooms (stems and all) rather fine. Peel and mince the shallot. In a heavy skillet, melt three tablespoons butter, add the shallot, push around for a moment, then pile in the mushrooms. Turn down the heat to low. It will take about half an hour for the mushrooms to cook: they will become very wet after a moment. You must push them around occasionally with a wooden spoon. They will be done when all their moisture has been driven off. They will look black and buttery.

Cook the bacon and crumble it; beat the eggs, add the cream, beat again. Place the bacon and duxelles in the bottom of the crust and then add the cream mixture.

The mushrooms will float to the top, rather, so push them down with a spoon so they are well-covered with the cream. Dot with about one tablespoon butter, place in a 350° oven, and bake for about forty minutes. Allow to cool thirty minutes before serving.

## Italian Quiche

3 links sweet Italian sausage  
Butter  
1 fine large ripe tomato  
3 small eggs  
1 cup heavy cream

1 eight-inch pie crust ready for use  
Freshly ground black pepper  
Chopped parsley

Slice the sausage rather thin and sauté it in a very small amount of butter until it is well cooked. Then drain it on absorbent paper and pat it dry.

Peel a tomato—first either dipping it into boiling water or holding it over a gas flame—core it, and squeeze out the seeds, then chop it coarsely. Cook it in a pan with a little butter until it is just beginning to soften. Beat the eggs. Add the cream and beat again.

Place the sausage and the tomato in the crust. Then sprinkle with freshly ground black pepper. Add the cream mixture, sprinkle with chopped parsley, and dot with about one tablespoon butter.

Place on a cookie sheet in a 350° oven and bake for forty minutes or until done, then allow to cool for thirty minutes before serving.

# Quiche Divan

3 small eggs
1 cup heavy cream
½ dozen thin slices of cooked
   broccoli, stalks and flowers
1 eight-inch pie crust ready for
   use

½ cup grated Gruyère cheese
1 cup cooked chopped chicken
   meat
1 tablespoon butter
Salt

Beat the eggs, add the cream, beat again.

Place the broccoli slices in the bottom of the crust. Cover with the cheese and then the chicken. Add a shake of salt. Pour over this the cream mixture, dot with butter, place on a cookie sheet in a 350° oven, and bake for forty minutes or until done. Cool at least thirty minutes before serving.

# Spinach Quiche

3 small eggs
1 cup heavy cream
1 pound fresh spinach
Salt and pepper

1 eight-inch pie crust ready for
   use
Pinch of mace
1 tablespoon butter

Beat the eggs, add the cream, and beat again.

Wash the spinach under running water, remove all the stems, pile the wet spinach into a largish pot, adding no water. Cook over a medium flame. Keep turning and stirring. In five minutes it will be done.

Drain the spinach thoroughly in a colander and then with a pair of scissors cut into tiny pieces. Season with salt and pepper.

Place the spinach in the crust, then add the cream mixture, sprinkle the top with mace, and dot with butter.

Place on a cookie sheet in a 350° oven and cook for forty minutes or until done. Allow to cool for thirty minutes before serving.

# Mousses

The Oxford French Dictionary, while specific enough on the meaning of "quiche," takes, it seems to me, a wildly scatter-shot aim at the word "mousse." "A Mousse," begins the O.F.D., "is a young sailor under sixteen years old, a cabin boy," which is, I must say, not what I had in mind.

Next, "mousse" is "moss," as in "a rolling stone gathers no . . ." and it is not until the third entry that we come upon this: "Froth, scum, foam, lather." And that's as close as we get.

I can only suppose that the editors of the O.F.D. were something less than gourmets, otherwise why the inclusion of that word "scum"? A chocolate lather is conceivable, as is a strawberry foam, but really, a lemon scum? Or is that something you pour over a donnish pudding?

*The two caviar mousses that follow are hors d'oeuvres, to be eaten on toast slices, with drinks.*

## Black Caviar Mousse

1 envelope unsweetened
  gelatin
1 cup chicken broth

3 small eggs, hard boiled
1 four-ounce jar black caviar
2 egg whites

Soften the gelatin in chicken broth and melt over heat. Pour into a bowl and allow to cool to room temperature.

Divide the hard-boiled eggs, whites and yolks, and rub each separately through a fine grater.

Scrape the caviar into the cooled chicken broth and with a fork stir gently until all the eggs are separated. Add the grated yolks and whites; stir to combine. Beat the egg whites until stiff and stir thoroughly into the caviar mixture.

Pour this into a ring mold which you have rinsed in cold water. Refrigerate at least four hours.

Unmold and decorate with watercress.

## Red Caviar Mousse

1 envelope unsweetened gelatin
¼ cup water
1 six-ounce jar red caviar

1 cup commercial sour cream
2 egg whites

Soften the gelatin in the water and melt over heat. Cool.

Mix the red caviar with the sour cream and add the gelatin. Stir.

Whip the egg whites until stiff and fold in thoroughly, then pour the mixture into a ring mold that you have rinsed in cold water. Refrigerate for at least four hours.

Unmold and decorate with watercress.

## Ham Mousse with Chicken Breasts

*Hot puréed string beans are good with this, with ripe cold pears as a finisher.*

| | |
|---|---|
| 4 whole chicken breasts, boned | 2½-ounce can deviled Virginia ham |
| Lemon slices | |
| 1 envelope unsweetened gelatin | 3 tablespoons mayonnaise |
| ½ cup chicken broth | 2 egg whites |

Cut the chicken breasts in two; poach them gently in water with a slice or two of lemon. They should be done in about ten minutes. Drain them, remove the skins, and place them side by side on the platter on which you will serve. Allow to cool.

Soften the gelatin in broth and then melt it over heat. Allow this also to cool. Mix the deviled ham with the mayonnaise; stir in the cooled gelatin. Beat the egg whites until they hold stiff peaks, then fold them thoroughly into the ham mixture.

Smooth a portion of the ham mixture over each chicken breast neatly, using all of it, and store in the refrigerator until completely cold and set.

### FOIE GRAS MOUSSE

A variation of the above mousse can be made by substituting a three-ounce jar of pâté de foie gras for the ham and mayonnaise. Put the foie gras through a potato ricer and proceed from there as above.

# Ham Mousse

*Serve this with Chinese pea pods, and end up with a water ice—
orange or lime.*

½ pound boiled ham                  1 cup chicken broth
½ pound cooked Virginia ham   6 egg whites
2 tablespoons mayonnaise
2 envelopes unsweetened
   gelatin

Grind the ham (use the coarsest blade). Place in a bowl and
mix with the mayonnaise.

Soften the gelatin in the chicken broth and melt over heat. Add
to the ham mixture, combine thoroughly, and allow to cool.

Beat the egg whites until stiff and then fold them carefully into
the mixture. Pile this into a serving dish—preferably a soufflé
dish—and allow to set in the refrigerator.

Some sort of sweet pickle mixture should be served with the
mousse.

# Cucumber Mousse

*Try this with a baked striped bass, boiled new potatoes, salad,
and Brie.*

2 envelopes unsweetened          1 medium-small onion, grated
   gelatin                              4 egg whites
2 cups chicken broth
2 medium cucumbers, peeled,
   seeded, and grated

Soften the gelatin in a half cup of the chicken broth and then melt over heat and allow to cool.

Heat the remaining chicken broth and then spoon into it the grated cucumbers and onion. Cook for not more than two minutes. Pour into a cold bowl, add the melted gelatin, stir, and cool thoroughly. Beat the egg whites until stiff, mix gently into the cucumber mixture, and pile into a ring mold which you have rinsed in cold water. Refrigerate two or three hours or until firmly set.

Unmold and fill the center of the ring with a bunch of watercress from which you have removed the stems.


## Lobster Mousse

*This needs only a Cucumber Salad (page 70) and cold melon slices for dessert.*

| | |
|---|---|
| 2 two-pound lobsters | Juice of 1 lime |
| 1 envelope unsweetened gelatin | ¼ cup heavy cream |
| 1 cup freshly-made mayonnaise | 3 egg whites |

Steam the lobsters for twenty minutes in about two inches of boiling water. Cool and remove the meat. Cut the tails into half-inch slices. Arrange the lobster meat on a serving platter.

Soften the gelatin in a little water and melt over heat. Cool.

Place the cup of freshly-made mayonnaise in a bowl, add the lime juice and cream and the gelatin. Combine thoroughly.

Whip the egg whites until stiff, fold into the mayonnaise, then drop the mixture in blobs over the lobster meat.

Cool thoroughly until set in the refrigerator.

# Shad-Roe Mousse

*You will have fresh asparagus, obviously, and then slices of plain Genoise cake (page 118).*

2 pairs shad roe                    1 cup chicken broth
1 envelope unsweetened gelatin   3 egg whites

Poach the shad roe in barely simmering water for seven or eight minutes. Drain and cool. Remove all membranes, and with a fork gently separate the eggs until you have as few lumps as possible.

Soften the gelatin in the chicken broth and then melt over heat and cool thoroughly. Add to the shad roe.

Beat the egg whites until stiff and fold them carefully into the other mixture. Pile this into either a ring mold or a fish mold which you have first rinsed in cold water.

Refrigerate until set, then unmold on a bed of chopped watercress leaves. Serve with freshly-made mayonnaise.

### VARIATIONS

You may vary this recipe by using a cup and a half of water-packed tuna fish. Be sure to flake it well. Or you can use cooked salmon, cooked crabmeat, or chopped cooked shrimp.

# Mousse of Sole with Watercress

*Start this meal with a hot Lemon Soup (page 104). After it, have homemade applesauce or an apricot purée with cookies.*

| | |
|---|---|
| 2 envelopes unsweetened gelatin | Butter |
| 2 cups chicken broth | 4 fillets of sole |
| 2 bunches watercress | 1 lemon |
| 3 tablespoons mayonnaise | 3 egg whites |

Soften the first envelope of unsweetened gelatin in a cup of chicken broth and melt over heat, then cool.

Remove the stems from the watercress and chop the leaves coarsely. Mix the gelatin with the mayonnaise and then fold in the watercress. Spread this mixture in the bottom of a nine-by-fourteen-inch serving dish which has about two-inch sides. Refrigerate until set.

Butter a flat pan. Lay the fillets of sole on it, squeeze a little lemon juice over each, and bake them in the oven until they are done—about twelve to fifteen minutes. Remove from oven and allow to cool thoroughly.

Soften the second envelope of gelatin in the remaining chicken broth, melt over heat, and cool.

When the fillets are cold, remove them carefully with a large spatula and place them side by side on top of the watercress mixture.

Whip the three egg whites until thick, fold into the gelatin and smooth evenly over the fish. Decorate with paper-thin slices of lemon. Cool in refrigerator until set.

In serving, be sure each person has a portion of the watercress along with his fish.

# Lemon Mousse with Strawberry Sauce

*Try this with a whole beef fillet, cucumbers sliced lengthwise and packed with lemon and butter, and a green salad.*

| | |
|---|---|
| Lemon peel | ¼ cup lemon juice |
| 1 cup heavy cream | 3 cups fresh ripe strawberries |
| 4 egg whites | Red currant jelly |
| ¾ cup confectioners' sugar | Kirsch |

There is a strange little instrument from France which, if you drag it over the skin of a lemon, will produce long minuscule shreds of peel. If you haven't one of these, slice the outside skin of a lemon in the finest julienne strips you can manage.

Whip the cream until it is stiff, then do the same thing with the egg whites. Combine these two with the confectioners' sugar, a little at a time, then add the lemon juice slowly, and finally the lemon peel.

Pile into a serving dish and put into the refrigerator to become very cold.

Hull and wash the strawberries and cut into fours. Mash about a cupful of them and place all in a serving bowl. Beat three tablespoons red currant jelly until smooth and place over the strawberries. Add a few dashes of kirsch. (If the strawberries aren't very sweet, sugar them.) Refrigerate.

Serve the lemon fluff in bowls and pass the strawberries.

# Strawberry Mousse

*To precede this: little baked chickens stuffed with mushrooms, brown rice, and a bit of grated onion. A chicory salad.*

4 cups strawberries
Sugar
1 pint best vanilla ice cream

1 cup heavy cream
3 egg whites

Wash and hull the strawberries and slice in half. Sprinkle them with sugar and refrigerate for several hours.

Allow the ice cream to soften in the refrigerator. *Soften,* not melt.

Whip the cream until it is stiff; do the same with the egg whites.

Combine the cream, the egg whites and the softened ice cream thoroughly, then add the strawberries and mix again.

Keep cold until ready to serve.

*A chocolate mousse is so adamantly rich, so loud in flavor, that it topples the balance of any but the strongest menu. And that pretty much means you will have a main course of beef.*

*So, for any of the following chocolate mousses, you might try Artichoke Bottoms with Hollandaise Sauce (page 131), roast beef, little browned potatoes, Puréed Red Peppers (page 132), and a plain green salad.*

## Chocolate Mousse I ~~4 times these!~~

6 ounces semi-sweet chocolate    4 tablespoons butter
2 ounces unsweetened chocolate    6 eggs, separated
¼ cup strong coffee    ½ cup heavy cream
   6 tablespoons sugar

In the top part of a double boiler over simmering water melt both chocolates along with the coffee, then stir in the butter. In a bowl beat the egg yolks until very light and pour the chocolate over them. Mix well. You must now let this cool.

Whip the cream and stir in the sugar. Beat the egg whites until they hold peaks, then carefully fold the cream and the egg whites into the chocolate mixture.

Refrigerate four or five hours.

## Chocolate Mousse II

6 ounces semi-sweet chocolate bits    1 cup light cream plus 3 tablespoons milk
1 ounce unsweetened chocolate    4 eggs, separated

In a blender place the semi-sweet chocolate bits and the unsweetened square, which you have chopped up a bit. Heat the light cream and the milk just to the boiling point, then pour it into the blender. Run the blender until the racket has stopped and the cream is extremely smooth. Then drop the egg yolks one by one into the still-running blender. Let run for a few seconds longer.

Pour into a bowl and allow to cool.

Beat the egg whites until stiff, then fold them thoroughly into the chocolate mixture.

Refrigerate four or five hours.


## Chocolate Mousse III

½ pound Maillard's triple va-    4 egg yolks
nilla sweet chocolate    1 cup heavy cream
1 cup light cream

Grate the chocolate and place it with the light cream in the top part of a double boiler over simmering water. Cook until smooth. In a bowl beat the egg yolks and pour the chocolate mixture over them. Combine well and cool.

Beat the heavy cream and fold into the chocolate mixture.

Refrigerate four or five hours.

# Chocolate Mousse IV

½ pound sweet chocolate, grated

1½ ounces unsweetened chocolate, grated

5 tablespoons coffee (liquid, that is)

6 egg yolks

1½ cups heavy cream

In the top part of a double boiler (over boiling water) melt the chocolates, which you have grated, with the coffee.

In a bowl beat the egg yolks thoroughly and pour the chocolate over them. Mix thoroughly. Allow to cool.

Whip the cream until stiff, then fold thoroughly into the chocolate mixture. Pour into a serving bowl. Refrigerate four or five hours.

You may wish to make the following additions to this mousse:

At the table, just before serving, pour a good dollop of crème de menthe over the mousse—about a quarter of a cup—and stir once or twice. Do not combine completely.


**VARIATIONS AND ADDITIONS**

Instead of the mint, try Grand Marnier or Armagnac.

Or chop up enough crystallized ginger to make half a cup, and swirl that in.

Or buy slivered almonds, toast them, chop them, and sprinkle the mousse with several heaping tablespoons of the slivered almonds. Or do the same thing with pecans or crumbled macaroons.

Of course, you may make any of the above additions after you have spooned the mousse into individual bowls. Perhaps better that way.

# Grand Marnier Mousse

*Have this finish off a dinner of fine veal stew with Homemade Noodles (page 112) and a Carrot Salad (page 69).*

3 eggs, separated 6 tablespoons Grand Marnier
3 tablespoons sugar 1 cup heavy cream
1 envelope unsweetened gelatin

Beat the egg yolks with the sugar until light and lemon-colored. Soften the gelatin in a little water and dissolve over heat. Cool.

When the gelatin is cool, combine it with the egg yolks and the Grand Marnier.

Beat the egg whites until stiff; also whip the heavy cream until stiff.

Combine egg whites with the Grand Marnier mixture, also half the whipped cream. Be sure the mixture is well amalgamated.

Pour into a ring mold which you have rinsed in cold water. Refrigerate at least three or four hours.

Serve with the remainder of the whipped cream.

# Raspberry Mousse

*Before this serve scallops of veal fried in lemon butter, mashed potatoes, and Celery Root Salad ( page 70).*

½  cup sugar
1  cup water
3  cups raspberries

1  envelope unsweetened gelatin
3  egg  whites
½  cup  heavy  cream

Boil the sugar and water for a few minutes to make a thin syrup. Add two cups of the raspberries and continue to boil for three minutes.

Pour the mixture into a blender and run until smooth, then pour into a bowl.

Soften the gelatin in a little water, then melt over heat and add to the raspberry mixture. Cool thoroughly.

Whip the egg whites until stiff, also the cream.

Combine the egg whites and the cream with the raspberry mixture thoroughly, then fold in the final cup of raspberries. Scrape this into a serving bowl and chill for several hours in the refrigerator.

## VARIATIONS

Ripe strawberries can be substituted for the raspberries; also fresh pineapple.

# Orange Mousse

*A good ending to a meal of Parsleyed Lamb (page 130), accompanied by its onions and potatoes, plus a simple salad.*

| | |
|---|---|
| 1 envelope unsweetened gelatin | Grated peel of one orange |
| ¼ cup cold water | 3 eggs, separated |
| 1 cup fresh orange juice | ½ cup sugar |
| 1 tablespoon cornstarch | ¼ cup heavy cream |

In a saucepan soften the envelope of gelatin in the water. After five minutes add the orange juice, the tablespoon of cornstarch, and the grated orange peel. Heat gently, stirring constantly until mixture has thickened slightly, about four minutes. Remove from fire.

In a bowl beat the egg yolks and the sugar until they are a light lemon color. Pour over them the orange juice–gelatin mixture and whisk to combine thoroughly. Cool to room temperature.

Beat the egg whites until stiff, then whip the cream. Combine with the orange mixture and pour into a ring mold which you have rinsed in cold water. Refrigerate for several hours.

A perfect sauce for this: Peel two oranges, take the skins off each section and place the pulp in a bowl. Add a half cup bitter English marmalade and a half cup Grand Marnier, mix together and place in the refrigerator for a long time—overnight is best.

To serve, whip three-quarters of a cup of heavy cream and, when you have unmolded the mousse, decorate with spoonfuls of the cream. Pass the sauce.

The
Random
Egg

If you would care for a statistic: we Americans consume sixty-four billion eggs a year, oh, give or take a billion or two. They are, obviously, a notable part of our diet. Most of them, I suppose, end up fried, scrambled, or boiled, but a certain number of billions are used, disguised, in everything from bread to ice cream to ladies' shampoos.

How many ways are there to do an egg? I would not hazard a guess. How many angels can stand on the head of a pin? Plenty, in both cases.

Following is a random smattering of recipes which require eggs. Some are old delights you may have forgotten, such as boiled custard; some are common commodities you may never have thought to try, such as homemade noodles.

Buy the freshest eggs you can find—brown, white, speckled, the color doesn't matter. And treat them with respect. Never leave an egg alone in the kitchen while it is cooking; if you are baking, always keep a nervous eye on the clock.

# Lemon Soup

| | |
|---|---|
| 6 cups chicken broth | 2 eggs |
| ⅓ cup raw rice | ½ cup lemon juice |

Bring the chicken broth to a boil, add the rice, turn down the heat, and simmer for fourteen minutes, covered.

Beat the eggs in a bowl until light; add a little of the boiling broth to them, and the lemon juice. Beat well.

At the end of the fourteen minutes remove the broth from the fire, pour the egg mixture into it, and beat well with a wire whisk.

This soup is good hot, but it is infinitely better icy cold with a good grind of white pepper over each portion.


# Velvet Soup

| | |
|---|---|
| 4 eggs | 12 small clams, drained of their |
| 5 cups of chicken broth | liquid |

In a bowl beat the eggs, then heat the chicken broth just to a boil and pour slowly over the eggs, beating all the time. Pour this mixture into a fireproof bowl.

You must fit this fireproof bowl into a roasting pan, or a steamer (with a cover) large enough to hold it—a turkey roasting pan should be perfect.

Pour into the pan a half inch of hot water; set the fireproof bowl in it, and cover. This can be cooked on the top of a stove, but the water must never be hotter than a simmer.

At the end of fifteen minutes add the clams, and poke them

down into the soup. At the end of another five minutes the custard should be completely set.

Serve hot.

## Pavese

FOR EACH PORTION:
Parmesan cheese
2 slices Italian bread

1½ cups consommé
1 egg

Sprinkle some of the cheese over the bread slices and place them under the broiler to toast.

In a shallow pan boil the consommé and poach the egg in it.

In a large soup plate place the toasted bread, lay the egg upon it, and cover all with the hot consommé. Sprinkle with more Parmesan.

## Tomato Pie

Herbed butter
French bread
2 large ripe tomatoes

Salt and pepper
6 eggs
1 pint heavy cream

Make herbed butter: Mash together three tablespoons soft butter with a tablespoon of minced parsley, a tablespoon of chopped chives, and the juice of half a lemon.

Slice thin enough French bread to cover the bottom of a buttered eleven-inch pie pan. Spread each of the slices with the herbed butter.

Peel the tomatoes, cut in rather thick slices, and cover the bread with them. Salt and pepper generously.

In a bowl, beat the eggs until well mixed, add the cream, stir again, then pour over the tomatoes.

Cook in a preheated 350° oven for about forty minutes or until the custard is set.

Serve hot.


## Eggs in Anchovy Cream

8  hard-boiled eggs        2  tablespoons anchovy paste
1  cup heavy cream

Shell the eggs; slice them in two lengthwise; remove the yolks.

Place the yolks, the cream, and the anchovy paste in a blender and run until smooth. Arrange the whites, cut side up, in a shallow ovenproof dish that you can bring to the table, and pour the cream mixture over them.

Place in a preheated 350° oven for about ten minutes, or until just beginning to bubble.


## Caviar Omelet

FOR EACH OMELETTE:    1  tablespoon  commercial  sour
2  eggs                     cream
Splash of water        1  tablespoon black caviar
Pat of butter

Break the eggs into a bowl; mix them with a splash of water—don't beat them too much.

Heat an omelet pan slowly, until it is hot all over. Then drop into it a pat of butter. When the butter is melted, add the eggs, and in a minute begin pulling the eggs from the sides of the pan back toward the middle, then tipping the pan to allow the runny parts to cook.

When the omelet is set, fold a third of it over upon itself, then slide the omelet onto a plate and, with a twist of your wrist, fold it again.

Mix the sour cream and the caviar together and dribble on top of the omelet.

You can use red caviar, but, oh, the difference.


## Eggs in Aspic

6 eggs mollet
2 cups chicken broth
2 cups beef bouillon

2 envelopes unsweetened
  gelatin
2–3 slices prosciutto

To make the eggs mollet: Place the eggs in a pan of cold water, bring to a boil, turn off the heat, and allow the eggs to stay in the water for another five minutes. Pour off the hot water and run cold over the eggs until they feel completely cool.

Now shell the eggs, but gently; the shells do not come off so easily as do those on hard-boiled eggs. Eggs mollet are still slightly soft in the center.

Mix together the chicken broth and beef bouillon. Soak the gelatin in a cup of the mixture for a few minutes, then boil the other three cups of the bouillon and pour the gelatin into it. Cook for a minute until gelatin is dissolved, remove from the fire, and cool.

Pour one tablespoon of the bouillon into each of six ramekins. Place them in the icebox to harden.

When they are solid cut six square or round sections of prosciutto, lay them on top of the hardened gelatin, lay an egg on each and cover with the remaining bouillon. Return to the refrigerator to set—at least three hours. Unmold and place on a bed of watercress.


## Hard-Boiled Eggs

Eggs, you know, are porous. If you let one stand long enough, in plain air, the inside will completely evaporate and you will have an empty egg. Well, it works the other way too. Eggs can absorb flavors.

If you will put a half-dozen eggs in a bowl with a truffle and left them stand in a cool place for two days, then hard-boil them, you will have delicately truffle-accented eggs. And you can still use the truffle for something else, although its power will be slightly diminished.

Alexandre Dumas always had his eggs boiled in a strong beef bouillon, which actually does give them a different taste from boiling in plain water.

If you like curry, try hard-boiling eggs this way: Mix two teaspoons curry powder in a pan of cold water, add the eggs, bring to a full boil, turn off the heat, and let the eggs remain in the water for ten or twelve minutes.

Plain hard-boiled eggs should be made exactly as above but without the seasoning.

# Poached Eggs Masked in Soufflé Mixture

6 tablespoons duxelles (see
  Mushroom Soufflé recipe,
  page 39)
6 poached eggs

Cheese Soufflé mixture (page
  13)

Place a tablespoon of duxelles in each of six individual cocottes.
Lay in each a poached egg.

Make the cheese-soufflé mixture up to the point where you are
ready to slide it into the soufflé baking dish. Heap several tablespoons of the mixture over each of the poached eggs.

Place the cocottes on a cookie tin and bake them in a 350°
preheated oven for eight or ten minutes, or until they are well
puffed and brown.

# Mirror Eggs

1½ teaspoons butter
2 eggs

Sprinkle of water

In a small heavy frying pan, melt the butter. Break the eggs
into the pan.

Dip your fingers in water and shake them off over the eggs.
Cover the pan and turn the heat to low.

As you can see, these are simply fried eggs. But the water turns
to steam and cooks the eggs more evenly, so that you don't get
tough whites and uncooked yellows. The French call them "mir-
ror," because the yolks take on an opaque look such as you see in
antique mirrors.

# Eggs in Potatoes

FOR EACH PORTION:

1 baking potato
Cream
Butter
Salt and pepper
1 egg

Bake the potato in a 350° oven for an hour; cut an oval piece from the top, carefully scoop out the pulp, mash it with a little cream, butter, salt, and pepper, then return it to the shell of the potato. Make an indentation in the mashed potatoes large enough to hold a raw egg.

Break the egg into the indentation, salt and pepper it, return it to a 350° oven and bake until the egg is set.

If you have a little leftover caviar, a spoonful of it over the egg, just before you eat it, is a nice addition.

### VARIATION

You can also put a poached egg into that indentation and cover the whole potato with several tablespoons of Mornay sauce —which is of course a white sauce flavored with cheese—and then return it to the oven to heat through.


# Eggs in Cream and Wine

6 artichoke bottoms
Slice of lemon
3 tablespoons butter
3 tablespoons flour
1 cup light cream
1 cup dry white wine
Salt and white pepper
6 hard-boiled eggs

I suppose you will use the canned artichoke bottoms. Rinse them thoroughly, poach them for seven or eight minutes in water with a slice of lemon, and remove with a slotted spoon. Drain and slice.

In the top part of a double boiler (over boiling water) melt the butter, add the flour, combine thoroughly, then add the cream and the wine, a little salt and white pepper. Stir constantly until you have a thick, creamy mixture.

Slice the hard-boiled eggs and add them and the artichoke bottoms to the sauce. Cook until thoroughly warm. Serve over toast.

## Spaghetti Carbonara

| | |
|---|---|
| 8 strips bacon | Freshly ground black pepper |
| 1 pound thin spaghetti | Freshly grated Parmesan cheese |
| 4 eggs | |

Fry the bacon until it is crisp, remove, and drain.

Cook the spaghetti in too much salted water until it is done, about eight minutes.

In a bowl, beat the eggs lightly.

When the spaghetti is done, drain it. Then place in a very hot bowl. Heat the bacon grease, pour over the spaghetti, crumble the bacon and add it, and then pour over the four eggs.

Lift the spaghetti with two forks until all is amalgamated and the eggs are set.

Serve in hot bowls with a grind of black pepper and the Parmesan.

# Piedmont Fondue

½ pound Fontina cheese
3 tablespoons unsalted butter
3 egg yolks

1 white truffle, hopefully (or more likely four large white mushroom caps, thinly sliced)

Soak the Fontina cheese for a couple of hours in cold milk, remove, drain, and chop.

In an enamel saucepan melt the butter, add the cheese, and stir with a wooden spoon until melted.

Beat the egg yolks, add to the cheese, and stir to combine thoroughly. Keep the heat low; this must never boil. At the last moment add the unlikely white truffles thinly sliced—or the more likely mushrooms. Serve over toast.

# Homemade Noodles

4 eggs
1 tablespoon olive oil

1 teaspoon salt
2½–3 cups flour

In a bowl beat the eggs, oil, and salt and begin adding flour. Add enough so that you have a good cohesive mass which you can handle with your hands. In other words, a good stiff dough. Form into a ball, wrap in wax paper, and place in the refrigerator for an hour or so.

Making noodles is extraordinarily simple if you will provide yourself with a noodle-making machine. These used to be hard to come by, but now you can buy them at almost any good hardware store. If you have such a machine, follow the instructions which come with it, then lay the noodles on clean towels or, in fact, on any clean surface, and allow to dry out. The noodles must be dry before you use them.

If you do not have a machine, divide your clump of dough into five or six pieces, flour well a large surface—a marble coffee table is perfect. Then roll out the dough with a well-floured rolling pin.

You must roll the dough till it is very thin—like silk. Next, cut the dough in very thin strips with either scissors or a sharp knife. Place these on towels and allow to dry thoroughly.

TO COOK: For four use half the amount of noodles you have made. (The rest can be stored in the refrigerator in a plastic bag —they will keep for several weeks.)

In a large pan of boiling salted water, place the noodles, and cook for no more than four or five minutes. Drain, then return to their hot pan, in which you have melted three tablespoons butter.

They are fine to eat plain, as is, but if you would like them at perfection, do this: heat one cup light cream just to the boiling point, pour over the noodles, and add a half cup freshly grated Parmesan cheese. Stir to combine. The noodles will miraculously absorb all of the cream.

# Irish Soda Bread

2 cups unbleached stone-
  ground flour
3 tablespoons unbolted whole-
  wheat flour

2 teaspoons baking powder
1 tablespoon salt
1 egg
1 cup milk

These natural flours can be bought at many places now, and certainly always at health-food stores.

First, butter an eight-inch spring-form pan or eight-inch round cake tin and place it in a 350° oven.

In a bowl mix the flours, the baking powder, and the salt.

Beat the egg lightly and add it and the milk to the flour. Combine thoroughly. You will have a thick, gummy mass.

Scrape the dough into the hot pan. Return to the oven and bake for one hour at 350°. This length of time is essential.

NOTE: You may use any combination of flours that suits you. Often in Ireland it is made almost entirely of the whole-wheat. Sometimes the egg is omitted and the milk is half water. Experiment until you find the loaf that pleases you most. Nothing can go wrong, however; this is never-fail bread.

# Yorkshire Pudding

Scant cup of flour                1  cup milk
1  teaspoon salt                   Butter or roast-beef drippings
2  eggs


Beat the first four ingredients together well with a wire whisk. Let stand at room temperature for an hour or two. Beat occasionally until bubbles appear.

This must be baked in a very hot receptacle. The classic way of course was to pour it around a roast beef, during the last half hour of cooking.

If you wish to make it separately, heat an eleven-inch round ovenproof shallow dish into which you have placed three or four tablespoons of butter or drippings from the beef. When the pan is hot, pour in the mixture. Bake for half an hour in a 350° oven.

NOTE: If you are cooking roast beef at the same time be sure that your oven will accommodate both pans.


**VARIATIONS**

You can give your Yorkshire pudding a slightly different taste by adding a half cup finely chopped parsley to the batter; another variation is half a cup of grated fresh onion.

The English Toad-in-the-Hole is made by first cooking a dozen little sausages, which you drain and then arrange in the batter just before placing the pan in the oven. Serve with Worcestershire sauce.

# Floating Island

| 4 eggs, separated | ½ cup sugar |
| 2 cups milk | 1 teaspoon vanilla extract |

Beat the egg whites until very stiff.

Heat the milk in a wide shallow saucepan.

Make nicely rounded spoonfuls of the egg whites and drop them onto the hot milk. Cook each of these meringues for a couple of minutes on one side and then for a couple of minutes on the other. When they are done, place them on a platter.

In a bowl, beat the egg yolks, add the sugar, and pour over them the hot milk; be sure you still have a pint; add more if necessary.

Pour the mixture into the top part of a double boiler over simmering water, and cook, stirring constantly, until the custard coats the spoon.

Remove from heat. Add the vanilla and cool.

### SAUCE

| ½ cup sugar | 3 tablespoons of Grand |
| 3 tablespoons strong black coffee | Marnier |

In a small, heavy iron skillet melt the sugar, stirring constantly, and cook until it is a rich brown. Take it off the fire and add the coffee and the Grand Marnier. Return to fire and cook until the mixture is smooth and slightly thickened.

To serve, give each guest several of the meringues with the hot syrup dribbled over them and surrounded by the cold custard.

## Boiled Custard

2 cups milk
4 egg yolks
¼ cup sugar

Pinch of salt
1 teaspoon grated lemon rind

Heat but do not boil the milk.

In a bowl beat the egg yolks, sugar, and salt. Pour over them the hot milk and stir to combine thoroughly.

Pour this mixture into the top part of a double boiler over simmering water. Keep stirring until the custard coats the spoon —just a few minutes.

Remove from heat, stir in lemon rind, and chill.


## Chocolate Pots-of-Cream

¼ cup milk
1 cup light cream
1 ounce (1 square) unsweetened chocolate

6 ounces semi-sweet chocolate
bits
4 egg yolks

Heat the milk and cream in a saucepan but do not boil.

Cut the square of unsweetened chocolate into smallish bits.

Pour the hot cream mixture into a blender and add the two chocolates; hold the cover of the blender on tight with your hand, and run until the racket has stopped and all is smooth. Add now the four egg yolks and run again for a moment.

Pour into six small ramekins, cool, then place in refrigerator for several hours. Remove from refrigerator at least an hour before serving.

## Vanilla Pots-of-Cream

½ cup sugar                      6 egg yolks
2 cups light cream
1 half-inch piece of vanilla
  bean

Place the sugar, cream, and the vanilla bean in a saucepan, bring almost to a boil, then set aside.

Beat the egg yolks until light, then pour over them the hot cream. Beat thoroughly with a whisk. Remove vanilla bean.

Pour equal parts of the mixture into six ramekins. Place in a baking pan with a cover. Fill the pan with a half inch of boiling water, cover, and bake in a 350° oven for about eighteen minutes, or until a knife inserted in the custard comes out clean. The custard is to be served cold.

This is a rather mild dessert. A bowl of crushed fresh raspberries helps it.

## Genoise

4 eggs, separated             2 teaspoons lemon juice
1 cup sugar                    1 teaspoon grated lemon peel
4 tablespoons melted butter
⅞ cup flour (1 cup less 2
  tablespoons)

Place the egg yolks in a bowl, beat them with a wire whisk, add the sugar, and continue to beat furiously with a whisk until the two are combined thoroughly and appear to have increased in bulk.

Melt the butter meanwhile and set it off the fire to cool. It must not be hot.

Add the flour to the egg-sugar mixture and mix extremely carefully. This must merely be mixed, never beaten.

Beat the egg whites until they hold peaks and add them with the same care. Next add the lemon juice, lemon peel, and the cooled liquid butter, again only commingling, never beating.

Flour and butter an eight-inch round spring-form pan, and scrape the batter into it. Bake in a 325° oven (preheated) for forty-five to fifty minutes. Test with a broom straw.

NOTE: This is not the classic fine Genoise, but is a good enough substitute. You can ice it, serve it with crushed fruit, or just eat it plain.

## Crepes

1 cup flour
½ teaspoon salt
3 eggs
7 teaspoons melted butter

2 tablespoons brandy
1 teaspoon grated lemon rind
1½ cups milk

Mix all these ingredients together in a bowl thoroughly, until you have a batter which is the consistency of thin cream. Or, better still, place everything in an electric blender and run until smooth.

This batter must rest—in the refrigerator—for at least four hours.

Ideally, to cook crepes you should have a crepe pan, which is a little six-inch frying pan with flaring sides, but any six-inch pan will do.

Heat the pan gently over medium heat, then add a thin slice of butter. Tip the pan in all directions so that the surface is covered with the butter. Next pour in a small amount of the batter, no more than two or three tablespoons, just enough so that when you again tip the pan in all directions the batter will thinly cover the surface of the skillet.

Cook for a couple of minutes, then with a spatula lift a corner of the crepe. If it is a pleasant brown flip it over, and cook the other side for only a minute or two.

Repeat the process until all the batter is used. This recipe should make twenty-four to twenty-six crepes.

NOTE: The above recipe is for entrée crepes; to make dessert crepes add a tablespoon of sugar.

The uses of crepes are infinite: you can stuff them with creamed lobster, creamed crabmeat, chicken, shrimps, mushrooms.

For dessert they are fine stuffed with chopped fresh fruit in a pastry cream; even plain applesauce wrapped in a crepe and then blazed with a little warm brandy makes a fine dessert.

And of course there are always Crepes Suzette. Here is a simple recipe for them:

## Crepes Suzette

| | |
|---|---|
| 5 tablespoons butter | ½ cup Grand Marnier |
| 4 tablespoons sugar | 1 teaspoon lemon juice |
| Finely grated rind of an orange | ½ cup brandy |
| ½ cup orange juice | Crepes |

The sauce is usually made at the table. You will need a Crepe Suzette pan, which you place over direct heat.

Cream the butter and sugar together. Then place in the pan and cook until well melted, then add all the other sauce ingredients except the brandy. When the sauce is bubbly place a crepe in it, let boil for a moment or two, then fold in four and shove to the side of the pan. Repeat the process with each crepe. This recipe will do for about a dozen crepes.

When you have finished pour the brandy over the crepes and light it. Serve each guest his crepes and spoon over each portion a bit of the flaming sauce.

# The Additional Recipes

# Onion-and-Cucumber Aspic

1½ cucumbers  
Salt and pepper  
2 medium sweet onions  
Pinch of fresh dill  
Pinch of parsley  

4 tablespoons olive oil  
1 tablespoon white vinegar  
1 envelope gelatin  
1 cup chicken broth  

Peel and slice the cucumbers very thin. Spread them on a platter and sprinkle liberally with salt. When they have begun to wilt—about an hour—wash them, pat them dry and place in a bowl. Add the onions, also sliced thin, the dill and parsley, the oil and vinegar. Combine well and let marinate for an hour.

Soften the gelatin in a little water, then heat the chicken broth and dissolve the gelatin in it. Rinse a ring mold in cold water. Pile the cucumber mixture into it, including all the dressing. Then pour over the chicken broth, which you have allowed to cool a little, naturally.

Give this time to set—three or four hours in the refrigerator; then unmold and decorate if you like with small hearts of lettuce.

# Horseradish Sherbet

1 cup sour cream
1 tablespoon lemon juice
1 tablespoon applesauce
Salt and white pepper

2 tablespoons freshly ground
horseradish, or 2 tablespoons
prepared horseradish—well
drained

Mix all these ingredients together and place in the freezing compartment of the refrigerator. Stir occasionally. It is ready when it is the consistency of a soft sherbet—about an hour and a half.

A spoonful of this makes a surprising accompaniment to hot Ground-Sirloin Soufflé (page 23).


# Mrs. Astor's Horseradish

*This is simply an accompaniment to anything that demands horse-radish—boiled beef, corned beef, roast beef. It's not bad with cold fowl, which is rather tasteless if unadorned.*

4 tablespoons freshly grated
horseradish
2 envelopes unsweetened
gelatin
1 cup chicken broth

1 cup commercial sour cream
1 tablespoon applesauce
1 tablespoon lemon juice
Salt
3 egg whites

You can use prepared horseradish if fresh is not available. Soften the gelatin in the chicken broth, then melt it over the heat and allow to cool. Mix together the horseradish, sour cream, applesauce, lemon juice, and a generous dash of salt, and finally the cooled gelatin mixture.

Beat the egg whites until they are stiff and fold them into the mixture gently.

Rinse a ring mold in cold water, pile the mixture into it, and allow to set in the refrigerator for two or three hours.

You may decorate this mold if you wish by laying thin strips of pimento at intervals across the mold before you pile in the horseradish.

## Crab Louis

¾ head iceberg lettuce
1 pound fresh crabmeat
1 lemon

3 or 4 tablespoons chili sauce
½ cup fresh mayonnaise

Remove the outer leaves of the head of lettuce. Then with a sharp carving knife cut the head in slices as thin as you can possibly manage. You will need about three-quarters of an average iceberg head. Shred this with your fingers and place in a large salad bowl.

Pick over crabmeat to remove bits of cartilage. Arrange the crab on top of the shredded lettuce, and just before you are ready to serve, squeeze the lemon over. Beat the chili sauce into the mayonnaise and mix thoroughly with the crab and lettuce.

## Chicken Breasts in Champagne Sauce

6 tablespoons butter
1 tablespoon olive oil
2 whole chicken breasts, boned and skinned

2 tablespoons flour
1 cup light cream
Salt and white pepper
1 cup best champagne

Heat five tablespoons of the butter with the olive oil gently in a largish enamel skillet. Lay in the chicken breasts and cook them over low heat for eight to twelve minutes, or until done.

Remove the breasts from the skillet, add the other tablespoon butter to the pan, and when it is melted remove from the fire and stir in the flour. Return to the fire, pour in the cream, add the salt and pepper, and stir constantly until you have a smooth sauce. Stir in the champagne. Return the chicken breasts to the sauce and let them simmer very gently for a few minutes.

Of course, drink the rest of the champagne.

## Whole Beef Fillet Larded with Foie Gras

Beef fillet for 4, in one piece          3 ounces pâté de fois gras

Be sure the beef fillet is not frozen and has never been frozen. Have the butcher trim off all hard fat and tissue.

Roast the fillet in a preheated 450° oven for twenty-five minutes (or thirty, if you don't want it too rare). When it is done, remove from the oven, and slice almost through into four. Spread a liberal amount of the foie gras between slices and then push the fillet back together again.

Place this under the broiler just long enough for it to get hot.

# Stuffed Leg of Young Veal

*This is a recipe given me by Marjorie Dell, and delicious it is.*

9-pound leg of veal, boned
Butter
½ pound prosciutto
1 pound fresh white mush-
   rooms, caps only, sliced

Salt and pepper
25 or 30 small white onions,
   peeled
2 cups best Chablis

Have the butcher weigh the leg of veal after he has boned it. You will probably have about six pounds, but be sure of the weight.

Flatten the meat and with a very sharp knife make a sideways cut along each of the long sides so that you have two pockets deep enough to stuff.

Into each of these pockets rub a little butter and stuff a slice or so of the prosciutto and a few of the mushroom caps. Then butter generously the inside surface of the leg, season with salt and pepper, and cover with the remaining prosciutto and mushrooms. Roll up the leg into its original shape and tie it in several places.

Melt four or five tablespoons butter in a large skillet and sauté the onions briefly in it. Now pour the onions and butter into a roasting pan. Lay the leg of veal on them, cover with the top of the roasting pan, and place in a 350° oven. The roast should cook for twenty-five minutes a pound, so make your calculation from the weight your butcher gave you.

For the last hour of cooking, take the cover off the roast and pour into the pan the two cups of Chablis. During this last hour baste frequently, at least five or six times.

# Parsleyed Lamb

| | |
|---|---|
| 8 large onions | 1 six-pound leg of lamb |
| ½ pound butter | Salt and pepper |
| 1 cup chopped fresh parsley | 1 cup white wine |
| ½ cup chopped fresh basil | 1 dozen small new potatoes |

Trim and peel the onions, but leave them whole. Soften one quarter of a pound of butter and mix it with the parsley and basil.

Trim as much fat from the lamb as you can, then make several deep incisions in the meat and force bits of the butter-parsley-basil mixture into them. Slather the remainder of the mixture over the top of the lamb.

Melt the other quarter of a pound of butter in a deep roasting pan which has a cover. Place the onions in the roasting pan and place the lamb on top of them. Season with salt and pepper.

Put the top on the roasting pan and place in a preheated 375° oven. Bake for one-half hour, then remove the cover and allow the lamb to brown for another half hour.

At the end of the hour, pour the cup of white wine over the lamb, replace the cover, and bake for a third half hour.

Boil the small new potatoes until done. Skin.

At the end of the third half hour, place the boiled potatoes around the lamb.

Replace cover and bake for final half hour. This makes two hours total baking time.

Remove the lamb to a platter, surround it with the onions and potatoes. Skim the lamb fat from the pan juices (or blot up with absorbent paper). Heat pan juices and serve as sauce.

# Artichoke Bottoms with Hollandaise Sauce

2 cans artichoke bottoms          Hollandaise sauce
1 cup chicken broth

Remove the artichoke bottoms from the cans, then separate carefully. Wash them thoroughly in cold running water. Heat the chicken broth, and poach the bottoms in it—just at a simmer—for six or seven minutes. Remove with a slotted spoon and allow to cool.

When ready to serve, cover the artichokes with the Hollandaise.


# Artichoke Bottoms Stuffed with Puréed Lettuce

1 can artichoke bottoms          Salt (optional)
1½ cups chicken broth
1 fair-sized head Bibb lettuce,
    split and washed

Drain and rinse the artichoke bottoms. Poach them in the chicken broth for five to six minutes. Remove with a slotted spoon and place in a shallow ovenproof dish.

Then poach the Bibb lettuce in the chicken broth for about five minutes, remove from the broth, drain, and swirl in the blender to a smooth purée. Taste it and add salt if you wish.

Fill each artichoke bottom with a tablespoon of the purée and add two or three tablespoons of that same chicken broth over all.

Place the dish in a 350° oven for ten minutes, or until it is hot.

## Carrots Vichy

3 cups scraped and very thinly     4 tablespoons butter
    sliced fresh carrots     Salt and white pepper

Place the carrots, butter, and salt and pepper in a heavy enamel pan and just barely cover with water. Bring to a boil, reduce the heat a little, and allow to boil until all the water has been driven off. By that time the buttery carrots should be cooked.

## Puréed Peas

4 cups raw fresh peas     Salt and pepper
3 tablespoons butter

Boil the peas in as little water as possible until they are just done. Drain them and pour into a blender. Run until you have a smooth purée. Scrape this purée into the top part of a double boiler (over boiling water), add the butter, salt, and pepper, and heat until the butter is melted and well combined with the peas.

## Puréed Red Peppers

4 bright red sweet peppers     Salt and white pepper
Butter     Tabasco

Core, seed, and chop coarsely the peppers. Drop them into rapidly boiling water and cook for only three or four minutes until they've just begun to soften. Drain them and pile into a blender. Run until you have a smooth purée.

Remove to the top part of a double boiler, stir in a couple of tablespoons butter, season with salt and white pepper and a drop or two of Tabasco. Heat over simmering water when ready to use.

## Potatoes Anna

| 4 medium potatoes, peeled and sliced very thin, then placed in a bowl of ice water | Soft butter<br>Salt and pepper |
|---|---|

Grease generously with butter a large round shallow ovenproof dish.

Dry the potato slices and cover the sides and bottom of the dish with a single layer of the potatoes. Smear butter on top of them and season with salt and pepper. Repeat these layers until you have used up all the slices, always using the butter, salt, and pepper.

Bake in a 350° oven until the potatoes have crisped—about thirty or forty minutes.

## Cold Curried Apples

| 1 cup sugar | 4 firm apples, peeled and sliced |
|---|---|
| 1½ cups water | thin |
| 2 tablespoons hot curry powder | |

Make a syrup by boiling the sugar, water, and curry powder until it thickens. Then reduce the heat and poach the apple slices, a few at a time, turning occasionally, until they have just begun to soften. You must keep testing them with a fork. Remove from the syrup and drain. They should be served very cold.


## Baked Bananas in Honey and Chutney

Butter

4 bananas, peeled and split
  lengthwise

4 tablespoons chutney, minced
  very fine

Honey

Grease a large shallow baking dish generously with the butter; lay the bananas in it, cut side up. Spread a little of the chutney on each and then pour over each a few drops of honey.

Bake in a 350° oven for fifteen or twenty minutes, or until the bananas have softened.

# Index

Noodles, homemade, 112

Omelet, caviar, 106
Onion
   -and-cucumber aspic, 125
   soufflé, 38
Orange
   mousse, 99
   soufflé, 47

Parsleyed lamb, 130
Pavese, 105
Peas, puréed, 132
Pepper(s)
   red, puréed, 132
   salad, 70
Pickled beets, 72
Piedmont fondue, 112
Pineapple mousse, 98
Poached eggs masked in soufflé
   mixture, 109
Potato(es)
   Anna, 133
   soufflé, 36
Pots-of-cream
   chocolate, 117
   vanilla, 118
Pudding, Yorkshire, 115

Quiche
   Alsatian, 74
   with anchovies and black olives,
     78
   crab, 74
   crusts for, 67-69
   Divan, 80
   DuBarry, 76
   with duxelles and bacon, 78
   Italian, 79
   lobster, 75
   Lorraine, 73
   with puréed chestnuts, 77
   spinach, 80
   with tuna fish and mushrooms, 76

Raspberry
   mousse, 98
   -strawberry soufflé, 50

Salad
   Belgian endive, 71
   carrot, 69
   cauliflower, 71
   celery root, 70
   cucumber, 70
   fresh mushroom, 72
   pepper, 70
   string bean, 71
   tomato, 71
   watercress, 72
   young lettuce, 70
Sauce
   caviar, 24
   strawberry, 46, 92
   vanilla ice cream, 55
Shad-roe mousse, 90
Shrimp-tomato soufflé, 19
Sherbet, horseradish, 126
Soda bread, Irish, 114
Sole
   mousse, with watercress, 91
   soufflé, 20
Soufflés (breakfast)
   bacon-and-eggs, 25
   blueberry buckwheat, 28
   chipped-beef, 27
   cornmeal, 29
Soufflés (dessert)
   apple, 52
   banana, 48
   chocolate
     with brandied macaroons, 61
     with candied cherries, 59
     Grand Marnier, 56
     with liqueur-filled chocolates,
       63
     -mint, 60
     -mocha, 58
     with pecans, 57
     plain, 55